Italo Emilio Canini

Four Centuries of Spanish Rule in Cuba

Italo Emilio Canini

Four Centuries of Spanish Rule in Cuba

ISBN/EAN: 9783337379216

Printed in Europe, USA, Canada, Australia, Japan

Cover: Foto ©ninafisch / pixelio.de

More available books at **www.hansebooks.com**

FOUR CENTURIES
OF
SPANISH RULE IN CUBA;
OR,
Why We Went to War with Spain

A HISTORICAL SKETCH

BY

ITALO EMILIO CANINI

WITH

Illustrations from Old and Modern Authorities

AND

The Latest Official Statistics about Cuba, Porto Rico, and the Philippines.

CHICAGO
LAIRD & LEE, PUBLISHERS
1898

CONTENTS.

Chapter.		Page
I.	The Discovery — Mistakes Made on Both Sides —The Siboneyes	13
II.	An Unpleasant Task—A Borrowed Glory—The Conclusions of Dr. Coke	1
III.	The Conquest—The Story of Hatuey—Los Malos Tratamientos—Girolamo Benzoni, and What He Saw—Father Montesino and Father Las Casas—Exeunt the Siboneyes	18
IV.	The Early Period—Adding Insult to Injury—Governors for Revenue Only—Corsairs and Pirates—The Storming of Havana by the Combined English and American Colonial Forces in 1762—The Events in the Latter Part of the 18th Century—The Dawn	32
V.	Thomas Jefferson and the Island of Cuba—The Designs of Napoleon—An Undeserved Compliment Unthankfully Received	43
VI.	The Secret Societies—Advances of Spain—The Policy of John Quincy Adams—Tacon and Lorenzo—The Decision of the Cortes—Why Tacon was Recalled	47
VII.	Narciso Lopez—The Expeditions of 1850-1851—The Martyrs at Fort Atares—El Garrote—As You Sow, So Shall You Reap	55

CONTENTS.

Chapter.   Page

VIII. A Plea for Lopez—The Influences at Play in 1850—The Real State of Opinion in the United States—The Message of President Buchanan and the Little Reason of Senator Brown—The Correspondence Between Secretary Marcy and Ministers Soule and Buchanan—Spanish Outrages—The Black Warrior—The Ostend Manifest—How It all Ended—The Wise and Honorable Conduct of the United States...................... 73

XI. The Ten Years' War in Cuba—Proclamation of Independence—General Dulce and the Volunteers — The Orders of Balmaseda — The Battle of La Sacra—A Reign of Terror—Pacification of the Island by General Martinez Campos—The Treaty of El Zanjon and How Spain Observed Its Provisions........ 96

XI. The Ten Years' War in the United States—The Sentiment in 1868—Cuban War News in 1869—The Wishes of General Grant—Resolutions That Were Not Adopted—The Filibustering Expeditions — The brigs "Mary Lowell," and the "Lizzie Major" — The Promises of Spain — The "Virginius" Affair — How Spain Abused the Patience and Forbearance of the United States...................... 109

XII. The Ten Years' War in Spain—Hopes That Were in Vain—King Amadeus, His Influence and His Abdication—A Modern Cicero—Emilio Castelar and the Genius of Spain..... 128

CONTENTS.

Chapter. Page

XII. The Golden Book of Cuba—The Execution of Leon and Medina—The Treachery of General Mena—A Distinction With a Difference —Two Cuban and One Italian Poets....... 135

XIII. Public Opinion Abroad—The Forests of Royal Palms Between New York and Washington —The Congressional Express—A Bouquet of Flowers From the Paris Figaro—Ignorance and Vitriol—How a Great Nation is Being Deceived 144

XIV. The Situation in Cuba After the Peace of El Zanjon—Outbreak of the Present Revolution —Jose Marti, His Work, His Death and His Burial—How Matters Stood in Cuba in April, 1898—The Brilliant Ideas of General Weyler—Why Autonomy is Not Acceptable. 156

XV. The Feeling at Home—Autonomy—The Situation in the Winter of 1897-98.............. 173

XVI. The Maine—The Outcome of a Commercial Inclination — Why Arbitration was not Resorted To — A Different Interpretation of Words—How Revolutions Should be Opposed—Freedom at Last—Why We Are At War With Spain—The Genius of America— The Future Destinies of Cuba............. 180

Notes ....Pages 197 to 209

Appendix .... " 210 " 215

The Climate, from Official Reports........ " 216 " 219

INTRODUCTION.

This sketch of the events which have taken place in the Island of Cuba since the discovery to our days has not the pretension of being an exhaustive history. It is an inquiry into the causes which have determined the present state of affairs, and into the reasons for which Spain, once the dominant power in the new world has gradually lost all her possessions, and has declined from her position in the front rank of nations, where the genius of Columbus had placed her, until now the pearl of the Antilles, one of the few last gems in her crown, and the most beautiful, is at the eve of being wrenched from her.

A few weeks ago Mr. Carl Schurz wrote the following lines: "If we go to war against Spain it is of high interest to the American people that their motives should be correctly understood by the civilized world." The truth of these words of the distinguished German-American statesman and publicist is apparent, and it becomes the duty of every American citizen to make himself acquainted with the circumstances which cause logic, reason and right to be on our side in the present conflict, so that he may, as far as it is in his power, be enabled to convince his fellow-men that the American

INTRODUCTION.

people have gone into this war for motives that are just and proper. With this end in view, in hope of bringing a modest contribution to the good cause, I have endeavored to ascertain what the policy of the United States and the feeling of the people of this country have been with regard to the Cuban question since its inception to the present date, and to relate the results of such a study truthfully and impartially.

I am indebted, for the facts on which this investigation is based, to the following authorities: Benzoni, Historia del Mondo Nuovo"—Southey, "Chronological History of the West Indies"—S. Doporto, in "Diccionario Enciclopedico Hispano-Americano"—Coke, "History of the West Indies" —Gomara, "Historia delle Indie Occidentali"— Ballou, "History of Cuba" and "Due South"—Kimball, "Cuba and the Cubans"—Murat Halstead, "The Story of Cuba"—and others. As regards the history of the last fifty years I have largely availed myself of such documents, American and European periodicals and newspapers, and other publications as I have been able to find in the libraries in this city.

ITALO EMILIO CANINI.

Chicago, May 25th, 1898.

SPAIN.

A scarred old snarling lion, with scraggy tattered
  mane,
His claws and teeth all broken, lies the ancient
  realm of Spain;
With the thirst for blood still on him, and still
  with hungry maw,
He rends poor bleeding Cuba, prostrate there
  beneath his paw.
He's a fierce and famed man-eater, and from early
  days of yore,
Has ravaged many an island, wasted many a teem-
  ing shore.
And the victims number millions whom his strength
  has overpowered,
Whom with ravening, bloody slaughter he has
  mangled and devoured;
But his roar grows faint and hollow, and a hunter
  from the West
Will snatch away fair Cuba, with her torn and
  bleeding breast,
And send him howling, limping, reviled of gods
  and men,
Back to growl midst bones and darkness in his
  mediæval den.
—From the *New York Tribune*.

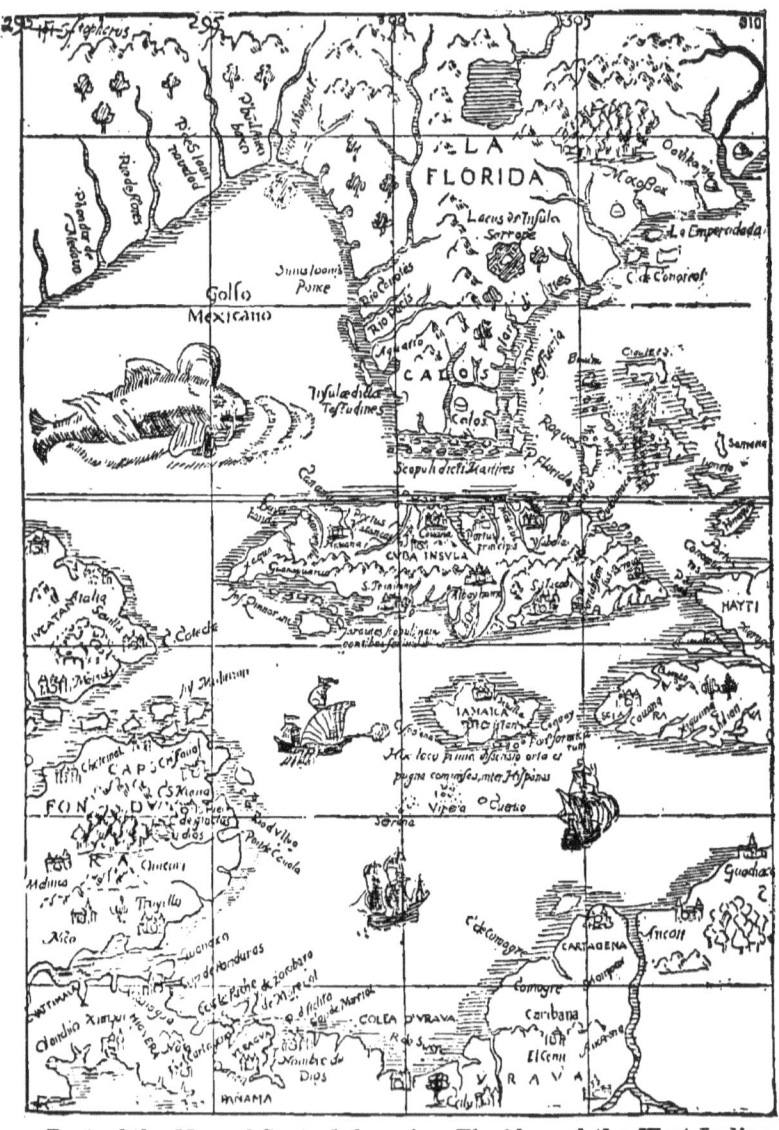

Part of the Map of Central America, Florida and the West Indies. Engraved at Francfort in 1594, by Theodore De Bry, for the Latin Edition of Girolamo Benzoni's Historia del Mondo Moro.

FOUR CENTURIES OF
SPANISH RULE IN CUBA.

CHAPTER I.

An Unpleasant Task—A Borrowed Glory—The Conclusions of Dr. Coke.

"History," said a great writer, "is a mixture of good and of evil, with here and there a glorious page."[1] But he who would undertake the study of the methods which Spain adopted in conquering the Island of Cuba, and in retaining its possession for four hundred years, with the expectation of finding such a page, would commit a grave error, for he will meet with the story of no deed on which he may dwell with satisfaction, and which may, perhaps, even cause him in a moment of thoughtless and quickly repressed enthusiasm, to congratulate himself that he is a member of the human race. The his-

---

[1] This sentiment, or one very much like it, has, I think, been expressed by F. D. Guerrazzi.

tory of Cuba is not pleasant. It makes one feel as if man were an animal very much inferior to a dog, and very little better than a tiger. It is, almost since the instant the foot of a white man first trod its soil until the present day, a tale of cruelty and corruption, of oppression and ferocity, which, for its continuity and its long duration, stands unequalled in the annals of the world, a monument of shame to the Spanish race, a blot on the conscience of humanity. It shows us that most of the evils of which that unfortunate island suffers at the end of the nineteenth century at the hands of its rulers, are the same under which it was groaning at the close of the sixteenth century, and that its lords have persisted from generation to generation in the same mismanagement and maladminstration, with the same blindness and obstinacy, learning no lesson from the past, seeking no improvement for the future.

"Spain," says Coke, in his "History of the West Indies," "has had the honor of discovering the new world, and the disgrace of murdering its inhab-

SPANISH RULE IN CUBA.   11

itants. The former of these deeds she effected through the genius of a daring and enlightened foreigner, but the latter through her own native spirit, trammelled by intellectual fetters, and accustomed to human blood;" and he concludes that "Spain has borrowed her glory and merited the detestation of mankind." Strong words these, but which, written, as they were, in 1808, have proved true to this day. Born four centuries ago in the blood of the native Siboneyes, Spanish rule in Cuba dies to-day in the blood of the reconcentrados; the former were burnt at the stake, the latter were starved to death.

She has exploited the seemingly inexhaustible resources of the island with the same greediness with which she exploited the gold mines in other parts of her American possessions, when in her anxiety to secure the coveted metal she cared nothing for the life of the miserable Indians who perished by the thousands under the burdens and the hard labor which she imposed on them during the course of the work.

Let us, at once, give Spain credit for what she has done. She has abolished slavery. She has not done it until a few years ago, it is true, and she was the last one of the civilized nations to do it, but— no matter how, or when, or why—she has done it. When this has been told, the only word that can relieve the story has been spoken.[1]

---

[1] See note 2, page 199.

CHAPTER II.

The Discovery—Mistakes Made on Both Sides—The Siboneyes.

The island which the Spaniards were to surname "the ever faithful," but which might better have been designated as the ever unhappy, was sighted by Columbus on the 27th of October 1492, and he effected a landing on it the following day. He gave it the name of Juana, and later it was called Ferdinanda, or Fernandina, then Santiago, and Ave Maria, but none of these names met with favor. The natives called it Cuba,[1] and it was under the Indian name that it came to be known generally.

On the first of November, Martin Alonzo Pinzon, who had been sent to investigate the surroundings of the landing place, reported that he understood that Cuba was a City, and the land a terra firma, and Columbus agreed with the captain of the Pinta in thinking that they had found the continent of India, and that they were about one hundred miles

---
[1] The Spanish pronunciation is "Kooba," with the b sounding almost like a v.

from its capital where he supposed that the Great Khan, or Emperor, resided. He sent three delegates to visit the interior of the country; they went a distance of twelve miles, then returned and reported that they had found a village containing fifty houses and one thousand inhabitants; the latter had received them with great joy, as being descended from heaven.

That joy was destined to be short-lived, and the opinion of the natives as to the origin of the visitors underwent, beyond doubt, a material change within a very brief period of time.

The race which Columbus found in Cuba appears to have been composed of the descendants of two nations that immigrated there before the Christian era, both coming from the southern portion of the North American continent. Part of the immigrants were called Nahcas, and were a branch of the Apalaches; others gave themselves the name of Caribs, and belonged originally to the Cofache nation. These immigrants displaced a prehistoric race which they found there, being probably a

SPANISH RULE IN CUBA. 15

branch of the Mayas, of Yucatan, or perhaps blended with it. At the time of the discovery the natives of Cuba called themselves Siboneyes.

While the Caribs, who then inhabited the Windward Islands were a fierce, warlike and ferocious people, practicing cannibalism, the Cubans, or Siboneyes, were on the contrary, a mild, gentle and docile race. The island was governed by nine Caciques, or Chiefs. Their religion was a belief in the immortality of the soul, and in the existence of one kind and beneficent God. Their priests, however, are said to have been cunning and fanatical, and given to exciting superstition among the people, in order to prey upon them. The "Historia Generale delle Indie Occidentali," written in Spanish by Francisco Lopez de Gomara, the Secretary to Hernan Cortez, and published in Italian in Rome in 1556, gives us some curious details about the wedding ceremonies of the Siboneyes. When the bridegroom was a cacique the *Droit du Seigneur* was exercised by all the caciques who had been invited to the bridal feast, or by all the merchants when he was a merchant, and by the cacique and some of the priests when he was a peasant; after this, says Gomara, "the bride was held in very high esteem and consideration."

In May 1494, Columbus, on his second trip, tried to ascertain whether Cuba was an island or not, but after coasting it for 335 leagues he became convinced that it was a continent, and ordered Fernan Perez de Luna, and four witnesses, to declare upon oath that it was the beginning of India, and the land which he had intended to find. It was only in 1508 that the mistake of Columbus was discovered, after a voyage of circumnavigation which lasted eight months, by Sebastiande Ocampo, whom the King of Spain had sent to investigate the matter. Vincent Yanez Pinzon also sailed around Cuba in the year 1510.

Father Bartholomew Las Casas.
(See note 3, page 199.)

CHAPTER III.

The Conquest—The Story of Hatuey—Los Malos Tratamientos—Girolamo Benzoni, and What He Saw—Father Montesino and Father Las Casas—Exeunt the Siboneyes.

"The lorde Diego Colon being Admirall and chiefe Governour of the new India sent one Iaymes Velasques to conquer the Ilande of Cuba in the yeare 1511, and gave unto him armour and other thinges necessarie," so we are informed by the "Pleasant Historie of the Conquest of the New India, now called New Spayne," translated from the Spanish of Gomara and published in London in 1578. Velasquez sailed from San Domingo with three hundred volunteers and seventy regulars, in four vessels. Father Bartholomew Las Casas, the apostle of the Indies, and Hernan Cortes, the future conqueror of Mexico, went with him. By that time the native Cubans had had an opportunity of becoming acquainted with the real character and disposition of the newcomers. Hatuey, a Cacique in whose do-

SPANISH RULE IN CUBA. 19

The Story of Hatuey.
From an Engraving in "Don Spiegel der Spaensche Tijrannije."
(Amsterdam, 1620.)

minions Velasquez landed, was originally from Hispaniola (Hayti) whence he had been compelled to flee in order to save his life from the slaughter which had been made of the natives by the Spaniards. When he heard that the latter were approaching his newly adopted country, he ordered his subjects to gather in haste all the gold they could find, to worship it as the God of the white men, and to throw it in the sea. He hoped, by this, that the Spaniards, not finding the metal that they were so anxious for, would not remain but would sail away at once. However he was mistaken, and this time he could not escape his fate. He was taken and burnt alive. At the stake, a Franciscan monk exhorted him to conversion, promising him the happiness of Paradise. Hatuey asked if any Spaniards were to be found there. "Only the good ones," said the monk. "The best are good for nothing," cried the Cacique. "I will not go where there is a chance of meeting one of them."

It has been said, in extenuation of the conduct of the Spaniards towards the Indians, that the spirit

SPANISH RULE IN CUBA. 21

of the age was harsh and intolerant, and that there are many instances of cruelty to the natives committed by other nations in the course of their conquests in the new world. While there is undoubtedly much truth in these statements, it is equally true that the instances referred to were isolated and individual cases, and that no such systematical wholesale extermination and wanton butchery of an inoffensive people, as were the natives of Cuba, (leaving out of the question the Indians of Central and South America) was ever committed by any other colonizing nation.

The number of natives, or Siboneyes, existing in Cuba in 1511 is variously estimated at from two hundred thousand to one million. Twenty years later only five thousand of them remained.

Severiano Doporto, in the "Diccionario Enciclopedico Hispano-Americano," in trying to excuse his countrymen, says that terrible accusations have been made against Spain for the disappearance of that race, without calculating that the phenomenon repeats itself in our sight, without the possibility of cruelty or oppression being alleged; and that the natives were destined to perish by virtue of the same mysterious law which causes the disappearance of the Maoris, the Kanucks, and other peoples, among which the North American Indians. He acknowledges however that the mortality was beyond doubt increased by the labors to which they were subjected, by slavery, and, he adds, rather naively, by *los malos tratamientos*—bad treatment. There is no mystery in the reason of the sudden vanishing of the Cuban natives, the facts are clear and easily understood, and we shall soon see what the bad treatment consisted of in reality. "Many Indians, besides," adds the Spanish writer, "took their own life."

Why did they do so? He does not say, but the answer to this question is given us in the "Historia del Mondo Nuovo" by Gerolamo Benzoni, of Milan, who in a spirit of adventure and, as he says, to see the new world, left Italy at the age of twenty-two, in 1541, and joined the Spanish expeditions. He writes as follows in his book, published in Venice in 1572. "They went in the woods in de-

SPANISH RULE IN CUBA. 23

The Indians Die by Their Own Hands.

"Indi saevitiae Hispanorum impatientes sibi ipsis manus violentas inferunt."

From an Engraving by Theodore DeBry, in the Latin edition of Benzoni's History of the New World.

(Francfort, 1594.)

spair, and hanged themselves, having previously killed their children, saying that it was better for them to die than to live so miserably, serving such wicked and ferocious robbers and tyrants."

History records with honor the name of Father Antonio Montesino, a Dominican monk, who protested against the atrocities which were being committed by his companions. In consequence of his efforts, an edict was published, in 1511, by which the Indians were declared free, and it was ordered that they should be treated as such; they were not to be flogged, or forced to carry burdens, or to work on Sunday. Spain was thus beginning, at that early date, that series of promises to the natives of the island which were to be forgotten almost as soon as made.

Father Bartholomew Las Casas, who perhaps owed his humane instincts to the French blood which was coursing through his veins, for his father, Francois Cazans, had been a Frenchman, declared in 1515 that the Spaniards had destroyed the Indians with great cruelty. "His writings," says

SPANISH RULE IN CUBA.   25

Raynal, "have branded his countrymen with a disgrace which time has not and will never efface." The Spaniards, said Las Casas, to whom later was given the title of "Protector General of the Indians," laid wagers which could with one thrust of a sword rip open an Indian's bowels, or cut off his head with the greatest dexterity; they burnt them at the stake thirteen at a time, in an infamous representation of the Christ and the twelve apostles, filling with bullets the mouths of the victims to prevent their cries.

It must be conceded that these are indeed *malos tratamientos*, and, in the face of these undeniable facts it is quite amusing to read the intensely patriotic, but altogether erratic, manifest recently issued by Governor Augusti of the Philippine Islands, in which, according to the report published in the "New York Herald" of April 28th, he says, referring to the people of the United States, "they (the Americans) have exterminated the natives of North America instead of giving them civilization and progress." These words, in the mouth of a Spaniard, constitute an exhibition of impudence that is sublime.

The protests of Las Casas moved the King of Spain to send in 1516 three fathers of the Order of St. Jerome to Cuba, to remedy abuses and to protect the Indians. The Caciques were told that they were free, and several excellent regulations were made for their welfare, but the promises, of course, came to naught. The three fathers did not accomplish much good, and seem to have developed an antagonism against Las Casas shortly after their arrival on the Island. Again, in 1528, the King repeated his orders that the Indians should be considered as free men; in 1532 it was ordered that no Indian should be marked in the face with irons; a few years later another edict was issued providing that no Indian should be made a slave, but that they should be treated as royal vassals to the crown of Castille; the Indians in Cuba were not to pay any tribute.

Bancroft, in his "History of Central America," quotes a number of laws which were made by the

SPANISH RULE IN CUBA.

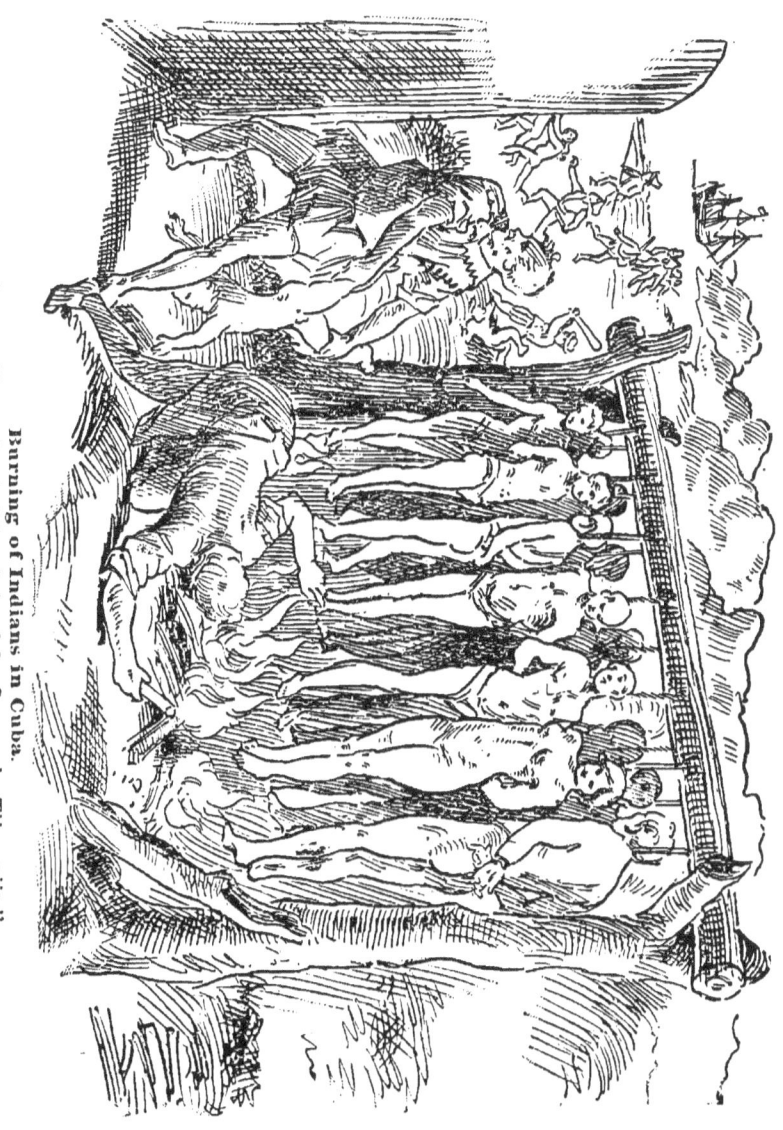

Burning of Indians in Cuba.
From an Engraving in "Den Spiegel der Spaensche Tijrannije."
(Amsterdam, 1620.)

Spanish kings in favor of the Indians, and he infers from them that "writers may possibly color their assertions, but by following the royal decrees we have what cannot be controverted;" he says that Isabella and her successors "stood manfully for the rights of the savages," but he admits, however, that "there were many ways the Spaniards had of evading the just and humane laws of their monarchs," and that "the evil proclivities of their subjects in the new world were of home engendering," due to the examples set by the monarchs themselves. We cannot agree with him when he says that the monarchs "protected earnestly, honestly, at the length of centuries," the natives of their colonies; more likely their orders were due to the intention of relieving themselves of the importunities of a few generous men like Montesino and Las Casas, and without any serious desire of compelling their subjects who, as Bancroft says, "went their way and executed their will with the natives," to observe the decrees; for it cannot be doubted that had they really intended to enforce the just and humane laws referred to

Cruelties of De Soto in Florida.

"Fernandus Sotto crudelitor in Florida Proefecturam exercet, abscissis etiam Cacicorum manibus."
From an Engraving by Theodore DeBry in the Latin edition of Benzoni's History of the New World.

above, ways and means of punishing the transgressors would not have been lacking. But Spain kept on signing edicts in favor of the Indians with one hand, and cutting their throats with the other.

We may surmise how, in fact, those laws were observed from the writings of the Italian Benzoni, who, as Southey, quoting from Humboldt, says, "relates the cruelties of which he was a witness with a sense of horror not to be found in the Spanish historians of that time." During the course of the expeditions in which he took part, in 1542, he saw the natives dragged to New Cadiz, to be marked on the forehead and arms, and to be played for at dice by the Spanish soldiers.

Sometimes the worm turned. The Indians took some of that gold which was the cause of all their sufferings, the desire for which had brought to their country the men who tortured and murdered them; they melted it and poured it red hot down the throat of some of their tormentors. This, however, did not happen in Cuba, for the natives there were too mild a race, and tame and incapable of resistance. Thus the unfortunate Siboneyes disappeared from the face of the earth, slaughtered almost like sheep by the strangers whom they had hailed as messengers of God.

CHAPTER IV.

The Early Period—Adding Insult to Injury—Governors for Revenue Only — Corsairs and Pirates — The Storming of Havana by the Combined English and American Colonial Forces in 1762—The Events in the Latter Part of the 18th Century—The Dawn.

The first settlement made by Velasquez, in 1512, was at Baracoa; Santiago, Havana, Bayamo, Puerto Principe and Sancti Spiritus were also founded at that time. The development of the Colonies, however, was hampered by the enmity which had come to exist between Velasquez and Cortes, and also because agriculture, which had been the basis of colonization, lacked hands and was reduced to naught. In 1523 the indigenous population was so diminished already that the importation of negroes began, three hundred slaves being brought to Cuba by advice of Las Casas, who thought he could save the Indian race by relieving the natives of the slavery and hard labors to which they had been subjected. This was the origin of the negro population of Cuba,

Herman Cortes.
From an Engraving in Henera's Historia General.
(Edition of 1728.)

which was to increase to such large proportions in the future.

The Spaniards lived in continual discord. De Soto moved from Cuba, in 1539, to the conquest of Florida, and his expedition further depopulated the country. In 1536 the first Corsair had made his appearance in the waters of Havana; he was a Frenchman, and he raised seven hundred ducats from the inhabitants who were frightened by his threat of burning the town. The next day he was chased by three Spanish vessels, but captured all three, and returning to Havana compelled the inhabitants to pay him seven hundred ducats more. In 1543 the residence of the Governor was established at Havana.

It is admitted by Spanish writers that the disorder which reigned in the administration of the Island, the corruption and cruelty of the Colons, the fanaticism and bigotry of the bishops, during the whole of the 16th century, could not have been greater. "The history of the Spanish administration of that time," says Doporto, "is shameful."

An examination of the accounts of Velasquez was ordered, or, as the Spanish expression is to denote the investigation of the conduct of a public official, he was *"residenciado"* by Zuazo, who replaced him as governor of the Colony, and was himself "residenciado" a few years later by Diego Colon, a son of the discoverer. The next governor, Juan Altamirano, came in 1525 to investigate the preceding administrations, and the same measure was adopted towards him when Guzman was sent to take his place. The latter being himself "residenciado" and substituted by Juan Vadillo. And so on; governor after governor succeeded each other, having been sent from Spain to inquire into the misdeeds of his predecessor, but the "residenciador," after having found out the methods and system of peculation which the former governor had carried on, instead of remedying the evils, simply used the information for his own benefit, adopting most likely such improvements in his own way of stealing and of imposing on the people as were suggested to him by the knowledge which he had acquired of the ex-

The La Cosa Vignette.
The only reproduction of the features of Columbus, drawn during his life.
(See note 1, page 197.)

perience of others, until he was himself "residenciado," by another man, who did the same. Several of these governors, among others one Gasparo de Torres, are acknowledged by Spanish writers to have been real bandits.

French corsairs continued to infest the island, one of them sacked Havana in 1543, in spite of the fortifications which had been erected. Drake presented himself before Havana in 1586, but the English fleet was defeated, shortly after, near the Isla de Pinos. At that time the construction of the Castles of Morro and of La Punta was begun. Santiago was fortified in 1630.

The population of Cuba was increased by fugitives from Jamaica after the latter had been conquered by the English, and reached 30,000 inhabitants, about 1650. In 1658, Puerto Principe and Santiago were sacked by pirates, also, shortly after, Puerto Principe for the second time, and Sancti Spiritus. During the whole of the 17th century contraband and piracy reigned supreme, and with almost absolute impunity; but the various governors who succeeded each other at the beginning of the 18th century erected stronger fortifications, and finally routed the corsairs and exterminated piracy.

Shortly after, the spirit of revolt of the Cubans of Spanish blood against the mother country asserted itself for the first time; riots broke out in Havana and Santiago, caused by several oppressive regulations of the government. Ogier, an English officer, threatened a landing in Havana, at that time, but finally desisted from his purpose. Hostilities having begun again between England and Spain, an English fleet under Admiral Vernon attempted the seizure of Santiago in 1741, but was repulsed. In 1762, however, the English, under Admiral Pococke and Lord Albemarle, stormed Havana, which capitulated on the 13th of August. Victory, perhaps, would not have been favorable to the English forces, or at any rate could only have been gained by them with much more difficulty, had it not been for the timely help given them by the reinforcements which they received at the end of July, consisting of about 2,300 men from New York, Connect-

Havana in the 16th Century.
From an Engraving in Montanus.

icut and New Jersey, under the command of General Lyman of Connecticut, and of Colonel Israel Putnam of New York.

The losses of the English during the siege which had begun early in June, were 1,790 men killed in battle, besides 700 who died of fever. All the territory conquered by England in the Island of Cuba was restored to Spain by virtue of Article 19 of the Treaty of Peace dated February 10th, 1763, between the kings of Britain, of France and of Spain.

After the conclusion of the peace with England the Spanish army in Cuba was reorganized by an Irishman named O'Reilly. At that time a regular mail service was established between Spain and her colonies, calling at Havana every three months. The taxes and tributes were considerably increased, causing disturbances which, however, were soon quelled, among the planters of Camaguey and of the Vuelta Abajo. In 1774, a census was taken of the population of the Island, and it was found to consist of 161,610 inhabitants, of whom 96,530 were whites and 71,180 negroes, including about 45,000 slaves. In

SPANISH RULE IN CUBA.

1792, another census was made, showing that the total population had increased to 272,000. Three years later the cession of Hayti to France caused the emigration of about 12,000 families from that Island to Cuba, and from that moment dates the beginning of the sugar industry in Cuba.

Although, as we have seen, riots and disturbances had taken place before, the real beginning of the bitter strife between the Spaniards and the native Cuban population may be assigned to the end of the 18th century, when the dissatisfaction of the native colonists against their rulers began to manifest itself in political and social contests, notwithstanding the fact that the administration of Luis de las Casas (1790) was the most tolerable that Cuba had ever had. But the spirit of the revolt of the thirteen colonies against the domination of England was abroad; its influence and that of the French Revolution were felt throughout the world, and caused the hearts of the oppressed to throb and their minds to awaken to new desires and hopes. The Cubans, then, began to show their opposition to many acts of the government, and to discuss and criticise the actions of the authorities. Even women took a lively part in the struggle, and those who were opposed to Spanish domination adopted the custom of cutting their hair, a curious way of showing their disaffection, but which served the purpose of distinguishing them from the women of the opposite party.

Thus it was that, in the last days of the dying century, a faint ray of light dawned above the darkness which had enveloped Cuba for wellnigh three hundred years, and by this gleam the precursors of "Cuba libre" read in the future the promise of a better day.

CHAPTER V.

Thomas Jefferson and the Island of Cuba—The Designs of Napoleon—An Undeserved Compliment Unthankfully Received.

The first evidence of the interest which the United States have ever since taken in the destinies of the neighboring island may be said to date from the time at which the purchase of Louisiana was proposed. It was at about that time, or shortly after, that Thomas Jefferson[1] thinking that Spain might be induced to cede Cuba as France agreed to cede Louisiana, wrote that Napoleon would certainly give his consent to our receiving the Floridas, and with some difficulty possibly Cuba. "I would," wrote Jefferson, "immediately erect a column in the southernmost limit of Cuba, and inscribe on it *Ne plus ultra*, as to us, in that direction. We should then have only to include the North in our confederacy, which would be, of course, after the first war, and we should have such an empire for Liberty

---
(1) Murat Halstead, "The Story of Cuba," page 28 and 29.

as She has never surveyed since the creation; and I am persuaded no constitution was ever before so well calculated as ours for extensive empire and self-government."

The fortifications of Cuba had been increased at the end of the 18th century by Governor Santa Clara, who feared an attack by England, but during the governorship of Somaruelos several coast towns were nevertheless assaulted and sacked by English corsairs. Somaruelos in arming the natives and encouraging them to resistance proclaimed that Englishmen being "no christians" were to be considered as enemies of mankind; which shows us that Augusti had some predecessors among his compatriots in the matter of making wild and extraordinary statements.

In 1808 news was brought to Havana by Juan de Aguilar of the movement initiated in Spain against the French. "Juntas," or Committees were organized for eventual defense; 6,000 unnaturalized Frenchmen were expelled from the island, not a few murdered, and many houses and plantations belonging to them or their sympathizers were destroyed.

These excesses were undoubtedly committed by the "Peninsulars," as the inhabitants of Cuba who are natives of Spain are called, to distinguish them from the natives of the Island, to whom the name of "Insulars" is given. It was among that same class, the Peninsulars, which at the present time is said to comprise about one-fifth of the white population, that the notorious Volunteers of the future Cuban revolutions were to be recruited. What the attitude of the real Cubans, the Insulars, was at that time, I have not been able to ascertain, but although the Cuban provincial council resolved that the island should remain devoted to the Bourbons, after they had been deposed by Napoleon, and although it recognized, in the same Resolution, Ferdinand VII. as king, I believe that the great mass of the genuine Cuban, the Insular, population merely remained passive. Perhaps the rather more liberal administration of Don Luis de las Casas had had an effect in that direction, but more likely the Cubans were simply indifferent before a prospective change of masters, although Heaven knows that they could not have fared worse.

The freedom of commerce was obtained through the exertions of Francisco de Arranjo, the most illustrious name, says Ballou, in Cuban history.

In 1810 Napoleon being anxious that Cuba should arise against Spain sent an emissary, Jose Aleman, to promote a revolution, but his man was captured and promptly hanged. After this, Spain decorated the island with the title of "the ever faithful," thinking, undoubtedly, that its bestowal was ample compensation for all past and future grievances. Cuba has ever since borne the new affliction with resignation, feeling much as a man would who being confined to a prison cell by four stone walls and a few iron bars hears himself praised for his good home-staying qualities. In 1814, possibly as a reward for her faithfulness, all such liberal concessions as she had enjoyed under the administration of Don Luis de las Casas, were suppressed by Ruiz de Apodaca, whom the "Bourbonesque" reaction sent as governor to the island in that year.

CHAPTER VI.

The Secret Societies—Advances of Spain—The Policy of John Quincy Adams—Tacon and Lorenzo—The Decision of the Cortes—Why Tacon was Recalled.

In 1820, we find the troops in Havana revolting against Governor Cagical and compelling him to proclaim the constitution of 1812; but its benefits did not last long and soon the reactionary party had everything its own way again. At about that time, and notably in 1823, a number of secret societies were formed, such as the "Soles de Bolivar," the "Society of the Black Eagle," and many others. Some of the authorities on Cuban history state that the former of these associations, and others, were merely established for the sake of amusement and of friendly intercourse among their members, but the opinion of other historians that they were intended for no such innocent purpose, and that all of them were organized in order to conspire for the independence of the islands is much more likely to be in accordance with the truth.

Spain, in 1825, offered some commercial advantages to the United States, on condition that the latter should guarantee the possession of Cuba to her, but the Spanish offers were refused. It was feared by the Spaniards that the people of the continent who had arisen against their domination would assist the Cubans by sending troops to the island in order to overthrow the power of the mother country; but the scheme of invasion of Cuba and Porto Rico by the combined forces of Mexico and Colombia was defeated by the opposition of the United States, who feared that Cuba instead of gaining its liberty would fall into the hands of another European power, a change which could, of course, on no account be permitted. John Quincy Adams, then President of the United States, said in a message that all our efforts would, for that reason, be directed "to preserve the existing state of things."

But another sentiment, besides the one contained in the recently proclaimed Monroe Doctrine, was at the bottom of that opposition. The policy of the

SPANISH RULE IN CUBA.

United States at that time was influenced, we must acknowledge it to our sorrow, by the fear that if Cuba should be liberated, or if any other power should get possession of it, the slaves might be set free, an event which the Southern States of this country considered as dangerous for the continuance of slavery in the United States. This ungenerous feeling, entirely contrary to the principles which have created this nation and made it what it is, was however in accordance with the prevalent desires of a part of the country at that time.

"The proximity of Cuba," says Henry Wilson, [1] "to the mouth of the Mississippi river, and its commanding position in the Gulf of Mexico, made that island a matter of interest and importance to the people of the United States, whether it was held by Spain, or was independent or free. Here, however, as everywhere else, the interests of slavery were made paramount, and the Slave power controlled the action of the government—a fact detrimental alike to the well-being and the honor of the Republic.

---

[1] Henry Wilson—"Rise and Fall of the Slave Power in America."

"When the Spanish Colonies in America became independent they abolished slavery. Apprehensive that the Republics of Mexico and Colombia would be anxious to wrest Cuba and Porto Rico from Spain, secure their independence and introduce into the islands the idea, if they did not establish the fact, of freedom, the Slave-masters at once sought to guard against what they deemed so calamitous an event."

"Thus clearly and unequivocally," adds Wilson, "did this Republic step forth the champion of slavery and boldly insist that those islands should remain under the hateful despotism of Spain rather than gain their independence by means that should inure to the detriment of its cherished system. Indeed, it would fight to fasten more securely the bondage on Cuba and the slave. Such was the purpose of the hour, and such the animating spirit of the national administration."

The same policy was continued during the administration of General Jackson, when representations were made by Mr. Van Buren against the sudden emancipation of a numerous slave population.

SPANISH RULE IN CUBA.

General Vives then suppressed the conspirations which had been formed in Puerto Principe and elsewhere, and crushed the insurrection which had been projected by the Societies. Several of these were composed of negroes, and in this, perhaps, lay the root of the fears which had been manifested in the United States.

The government of the Island passed at that time into the hands of General Tacon, the Eastern Department being commanded by General Lorenzo. The latter, in 1836, was in Santiago, and on receiving notice that the Queen Regent of Spain had taken oath to the Constitution of 1812, he, without waiting for the orders of his chief, immediately proclaimed through his Department that the benefits of the Constitution would be extended to the Island, and granted a national militia, the liberty of the press, and other free institutions.

Tacon, who bitterly opposed the innovations, was furious at Lorenzo's action and moved against him with his troops. Lorenzo did not fight, but returned to Spain. The governor then established a military commission which persecuted cruelly all those who had obeyed the example of Lorenzo and had taken oath to the Constitution; some were imprisoned, others banished, even the soldiers who had merely obeyed the order of their officers in swearing to the Constitution were punished, 500 of them being condemned to work in the streets of Havana with their feet shackled. Tacon, fully satisfied with his work, enjoyed his triumph in the cause of tyranny, and awaited the decision of the home government in the quarrel between himself and Lorenzo.

This is how Spain settled the matter: "The Cortes,"[1] said the resolutions which they adopted— "The Cortes using the power which is conceded them by the Constitution, have decreed: not being in a position to apply the Constitution which has been adopted for the Peninsula and adjacencies to the Ultra-Marine provinces of America and Asia, these shall be ruled and administered by special laws appropriate to their respective situations and

---

[1] Murat Halstead—"The Story of Cuba," page 61.

SPANISH RULE IN CUBA.

circumstances, and proper to cause their happiness, consequently the deputies for the designated provinces are not to take their seats in the present Cortes."

And thus it has been ever since, and is now at the present time; the "special laws" for the Colonies of Spain, "proper to cause their happiness" were then Tacon's own sweet will, and have been since the will of Balmaseda, of Weyler and of others of that ilk; for under the Commissions which the governors received from Spain, Cuba has practically been in a continual state of siege. By a strange fatality, whenever Spain has enjoyed a more liberal administration at home she has never felt as "being in a position" to extend its benefits to her dependencies.

Tacon, after his victory, continued for a time in the government of the Island. It is on record that he built the finest theatre that Havana had ever had and which bears his name to this day; its splendors, however, do not seem to have caused the Cubans to forget their troubles. Incidentally, he did not fail to follow the example set by a long line of predecessors and to fill his own exchequer at the expense of that of Spain and of the pockets of the inhabitants of Cuba, both Insular and Peninsular. In fact he went at it so fast and so furiously, that at last he came to grief.

Spain had never intended that the governors she sent to Cuba should administer the Island for the benefit of the Cubans; they were sent to raise revenue for the crown, and as a reward for political or other service, merely as an opportunity to enrich themselves at the expense of the colonists, and with the understanding that they might squeeze them for that purpose. Tacon entered into the execution of the second part of this programme with such an enthusiasm that perhaps he forgot the first one entirely. Governor after governor had grown wealthy in Cuba, but this particular Captain General kept such a pace and acted with such a disregard of conventionalities that Spain probably feared that after he got through there would not be anything worth having left in the Island for anyone else.

Tacon was recalled.

CHAPTER VII.

Narciso Lopez—The Expeditions of 1850-1851—The Martyrs of Fort Atares—El Garrote—As You Sow, So Shall You Reap.

General O'Donnell, in 1839, discovered a conspiration, the object of which was, it is said, to liberate the slaves, and he repressed it. The separatist group, however,—or secessionists—had come, as a natural result of Tacon's tyranny and robbery, to constitute a strong and well-organized party, and it was beginning to find favor and sympathy in the United States; still the governor and the government showed themselves disinclined to grant any reforms. Outbreaks among the negroes occurred in 1844 at Matanzas, and again in 1848. But it was not till two years later that the first well defined, open and organized attempt at revolt against the Spanish yoke was made; at its head was Narciso Lopez, a man who was to become the first martyr for the independence of his country, and whose memory all Cuban patriots, and all lovers of

Narciso Lopez.

SPANISH RULE IN CUBA.

liberty, to whatever nationality they may belong, should respect and revere.

Narciso Lopez was born in the year 1798, or 1799, in Venezuela, then a colony belonging to Spain. His father was a wealthy landed proprietor, owning large estates on the "llanos," or plains, of that country. According to the usual life of the llanos, Narciso passed almost from the cradle to the saddle, or rather to the unsaddled back of a wild horse.

When he reached the age of fifteen, an event occurred which caused him to enter the military profession, although, it is said, much against his previous wishes and inclinations. Civil war was then desolating the Spanish South-American provinces, and through its operations his father had been deprived of nearly his entire property, or had seen it rendered unproductive and useless. With such means as he was able to realize Lopez established himself in business in Caracas, and his son, although a mere boy, assisted him by managing a branch located in the town of Valencia, in the interior of the country. It was then, in the year 1814, that Bolivar, the celebrated liberator of Colombia, fought and lost the great battle of La Puerta; in order to protect his own retreat he induced the inhabitants and the garrison of Valencia to make a desperate resistance against the Spanish forces, by promising that he would come to their rescue, a promise which however he failed to keep. The place fell into the hands of the Spaniards after a siege of three weeks' duration. It is said that Narciso, though so very young, showed the metal of which he was made, for he not only took an active part in the fight, in the ranks of the Valencians, but he even came to be recognized by soldiers and citizens as their leader *de facto* among the men who had collected at the particular point which he was defending.

The two Lopezes managed to escape from the horrible slaughter which, of course, followed the Spanish victory, but Narciso in indignation and disgust at Bolivar's action—unworthy, indeed, of the great patriot—and having lost all he possessed, joined as a private the Spanish army under the command of

SPANISH RULE IN CUBA.

General Moralez; so that by force of circumstances he was thrown on the Spanish side of that civil war, and in doing so he was fully justified by the whole population of Valencia, or by such part of it as remained, which naturally felt very bitterly towards Bolivar and would undoubtedly have shot him if he had fallen into their hands.

At the end of the war, after the evacuation of Caracas, in 1823, Lopez who had during its course given many proofs of courage, and had highly distinguished himself on several occasions, had reached the rank of Colonel. It may be noted to his honor that he was influential in causing the Spanish Ceneral to desist from his purpose of protracting the fight against the South Americans, and in consequence of his services in that direction he was invited by the patriot government to enter its service with the same rank which he held in the Spanish army. However he did not accept the offer and retired to Cuba in 1823. There, after abandoning the service, he married, and established himself, and thenceforward he was a Cuban. During the governorship of General Tacon he was accused of conspiring for the independence of the Colony, for the reason, chiefly, that during a dinner he had proposed a toast to that sentiment; he was subjected to a trial, but was acquitted.

Several years later, he happened to be at Madrid at the time that the Royal or Absolutist party, composed of the friends of Don Carlos, was threatening to upset the liberal government of Queen Christina, and he took an active part in the execution of the measures which were adopted by the Queen in disarming the Royalists of the Capital, leading bodies of the people in the operations to that effect. He was then induced to re-enter the army and to join the Liberal party in its fight against the Carlists; at the close of the war he found himself a General.

During the popular insurrection which took place afterwards, and which resulted in the expulsion of Queen Christina, General Lopez by the desire of the people assumed the command of the capital, as Governor of Madrid, and also became the chief of the National guard; afterwards he filled other offices, among them that of Senator.

In the course of these events, however, Lopez never forgot his affection for Cuba, his adopted country, and, secretly fondling the resolution of becoming its liberator, he finally resigned from the Senate in order to return to the Island. It was with great difficulty that the government gave him the permission of doing so, as his influence there was feared, but he finally obtained it through his friendship with Espartero,[1] and he returned to Cuba in 1839.

Lopez did not immediately begin to carry his schemes into execution, as he was bound by ties of intimate friendship with Valdes, then Captain General of the Island; but after the latter had been recalled, he at once began to make preparations in order to educate the Cuban people up to the ideas of liberty and independence which he cherished.

With that purpose in view and by undertaking the working of an abandoned copper mine, he mixed

---
[1] A Spanish general and statesman, prominent in the history of his country during that period.

with the peasants, the "Guajiros," as they were called. He dispensed medical advice and medicines, being guided by a French manual of practice which he had read; in fact, he became one of them, dressed in their own costume, and in many ways succeeded in making himself familiar among them. Having gradually inspired them with his hopes and aspirations, he became confident that the entire region would rise against the Spanish oppressors at the call of his voice. In 1848, he judged that the proper time had arrived but was induced to await the result of some communications which had been entered into with an American officer who was then in Mexico.[1] The delay led, through an accident, to the discovery of his plan by the government. His friends were arrested, but he succeeded in making his escape by embarking on a vessel called the Neptune, which landed him at Bristol, R. I. His plan, from the first, had always been independence, and then annexation to the United States.

---

[1] Probably W. S. Crittenden, a graduate of West Point, who took a prominent part in the Mexican war, although he was then only 23 years old. Afterwards he was shot by the Spaniards at Fort Atares.

SPANISH RULE IN CUBA.

Such was the man who became the initiator of that struggle for Cuban liberty which, though now and then interrupted, or baffled, may be said to have continued until the present time.

Lopez sailed from a port in the United States in the steamer "Creole" in the spring of 1850. The "Creole" was cleared for the Island of Mugeres off the coast of Yucatan, where Lopez arrived on the 15th of May, and he concentrated there three divisions, comprising in all 609 men. Thence he moved on Cardenas, and captured the town; but the Spanish government, through its extensive system of espionage in the United States, had been informed of all his movements before he left this country. Lopez had to withdraw in front of the large number of troops which he found ready to meet his expedition and was compelled to abandon Cardenas. With what was left of his forces he re-embarked on the Creole, and left the town, with the Spanish man-of-war Pizarro in close pursuit. The latter, however, was not able to catch him, and he arrived safely in this country.

He was arrested at Savannah on the 27th of May, but the District Judge before whom he was brought with many other members of the expedition refused to grant the time which the prosecution asked for in order to produce evidence against him, and he was discharged amidst the cheers of the people. He was re-arrested on the 15th of July on the charge of violating the Act of 1818, which forbid the fitting out or arming in our ports of ships to be used against any "foreign Prince, Colony, District or people" with whom we were at peace.[1] He was tried with a number of his companions, but the prosecution was finally abandoned.

The funeral oration on this expedition was pronounced by Queen Isabella in her speech from the throne at the opening of the Spanish Cortes, on the 31st of October, 1850. "Tranquillity," said the Queen, "was for a moment disturbed in Cuba by a set of foreign pirates who fled before the loyalty of the people and the bravery of the troops."

The "foreign pirates" were the brave American

---

[1] The qualifying words had been introduced into that Act for the specific purpose of including the Spanish Colonies in South America, then in revolt against Spain.

citizens who had generously offered their blood for the redemption of Cuba.

An insurrection headed by a patriot named Aguero took place in Camaguey early in 1851, but was defeated, and its leaders were put to death.

Fort Atares, in Havana Harbor.

A second expedition was undertaken by Lopez in the summer of 1851. He started for Cuba from New Orleans, with about 500 men, in the steamer Pampero, and landed at Morrillo, in Bahia Honda; but this unfortunate enterprise was doomed to failure since its inception, for here again the Spanish spies had faithfully performed their task. Long before Lopez sailed the Governor General of Cuba had had timely notice of every movement he was to make; letters were sent to him bearing the forged signatures of several Cuban patriots, arranging for a landing just at Morrillo, so that on his arrival there he found the Spanish forces waiting for him; thus he was betrayed and trapped.

After the inevitable defeat which followed his fight with the troops which, as a Spanish writer says, General Concha moved against him "with an admirable activity," Lopez, wandering on foot, attenuated by fatigue and hunger, was captured through the operations of a Spanish spy named Castaneda, at Los Pinos de Rangel, on the 29th of August, 1851.

Fifty of his companions, among them the American officer Crittenden, were shot at Port Atares, in Havana harbor; scores of others were loaded with chains and sent to prisons in Spain. Among the prisoners were, besides the Americans, many Englishmen and Germans. The English Consul showed the utmost kindness to his compatriots and comforted them to the best of his ability; the officers of a German society of Havana did the same for their countrymen. As to the American consul he told the American prisoners that they had placed themselves outside the pale of the law, and that he could do nothing for them.

It was true; they were outside the pale of the law, such as it was—And still . . . we are at liberty to believe that had a man of the stamp of Colonel Fitzhugh Lee been the consul of the United States in Havana at that time, the unkind and ungenerous words would not have been spoken.

Lopez, who on landing at Morrillo had stooped and kissed the earth of his country, asked for the death of a soldier, "los cuatro golpes"—the four shots, but even this was refused him, and he died by the garrote, at Havana, on the 1st of September. The last words of this hero were "I die for my beloved Cuba."

The garrote is an instrument of execution the

use of which is especial to Spain. We give here two engravings on which it is shown.[1] One of the engravings is a top view of the iron work of the garrote. It is attached to the upper part of a post about three feet in height. The principal feature

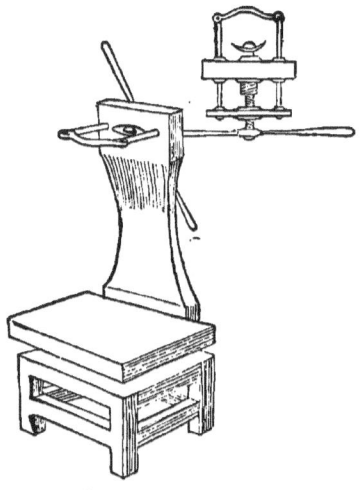

"El Garrote vil."

is a peculiarly threaded screw; one-half is left handed, the other is right handed. The front half of the screw passes through the post and turns in a nut fixed in the latter. About an inch from the end there is a curved piece to fit the back of the

[1] Both the engravings and the description which follows are taken from "Harper's Weekly" for May 8th, 1869.

SPANISH RULE IN CUBA.

neck. The end of the screw is somewhat rounded. To the back half of the screw a cross bar is fitted; from the ends of this two rods pass through holes in the post. To the end of one a semi-circular cravat of iron is hinged so that it can be closed upon the end of the other rod and pinned to it. A half turn of the screw will draw back the cravat by means of the left hand screw, cross bar and rods, while at the same time the point and curved piece will be thrown forward an equal distance. There is a seat attached to the post which is so adjusted that the point of the screw will come against a particular portion of the spine. When the culprit[1] is seated the cravat is closed and pinned, and at a given signal the executioner gives a quick turn to the screw. The spine is broken, and death follows.

The sentence of the court is usually death by "El Garrote vil." [2] By the old law if a nobleman is to be executed the sentence must be by the "Garrote noble." The only difference is that in the first case the platform is not sheltered or its floor covered,

---
(1) *Culprit* is the word used by the Editor of Harper's Weekly.—In most cases *victim* or *martyr* would be a more appropriate one.
(2) The low, or cowardly, garrote.

while the nobleman can demand to have a roof over him and his feet rest on a carpet.⁽¹⁾ There is but one garrote in each Department, and when required at any place it is sent under an escort of soldiers, together with the executioner.⁽²⁾

Lopez who gave up fortune, position and honors for his ideal of liberty; Lopez entitled by the nobility of his actions to be placed on the roll of those who sacrificed their lives for their country, was not entitled by nobility of birth to a nobleman's privilege, and therefore he died by the "garrote vil."

"History," says Molmenti,⁽³⁾ "is made by means of comparisons."

Mark the wise and generous policy adopted at the end of the struggle by the victors towards the vanquished, both towards the leaders and the privates in the ranks of the long and terrible civil war which only thirty-five years ago desolated this country. Contrast it with the conduct of a nation which by

---

(1) This is not due to a proper regard for the health of the occupant of the chair, but is in deference to the peculiar sense of dignity and honor which forms part of the Spanish character.
(2) The Editor of "Harper's Weekly" wrote this in May 1869, but undoubtedly since that time the rush of business must have caused an increase in the number both of garrotes and of executioners.
(3) Pompeo Molmenti—"History of Venice in private life."

its barbarism in this nineteenth century dishonors the old and glorious Latin Race, and observe the results. Here, a people compact, united, inseparable, strong in the faith of its future destinies; there another, drowning in a sea of blood, horror and abomination which it has itself created, and which as far as it extends to this hemisphere, at least, can be wiped out of existence only by the interference of the powerful arm of the North American Republic.

It is said that a Spanish diplomat, at the outset of the present conflict, stated that he entertained great hopes that by fomenting the old enmity of the Southern States of this Union against the Northern, much advantage would be obtained for the cause of Spain. What an utter, undescribable ignorance this statement which was ridiculed East and West, North and South, from Maine to Oregon, from the land of the Dacotas to the land of the Seminoles, shows of the true feelings of the American people and of the real state of affairs in the American Union! Grant and his advisers sowed generosity and mercy, and reaped gratefulness and forgetfulness of all past differences. Spain for four centuries sowed death, ruin and desolation, and she is now reaping desolation, ruin and death.

VIII.

A Plea for Lopez—The Influences at Play in 1850—The Real State of Opinion in the United States—The Message of President Buchanan and the Little Reason of Senator Brown—The Correspondence Between Secretary Marcy and Ministers Soule and Buchanan—Spanish Outrages—The Black Warrior—The Ostend Manifest—How It all Ended—The Wise and Honorable Conduct of the United States.

The two expeditions of Lopez met with failure first because he was betrayed by the spies of Spain who infested this country at that time, have infested it ever since and infest it to-day more than ever, and for this still more potent reason that the times were not ripe.

The most interesting work which was published about two years ago by Murat Halstead under the title of "The Story of Cuba," contains the following passage: "Reference is had in Wilson's History to the ill-fated Lopez expedition, which was of course in the interest of the formation of more Slave States in the United States, and it was that influence that made the most of the tragedy." In another part of the same work the author says: "The Cuban filibustering expeditions of a former generation, attended as they were with the loss of valued lives and the transmission of an inheritance of excitements and hatreds, were distinctly to provide for the admission of more Slave States in the American Union."

This is not a fair way of stating the case, because it casts on Lopez a shadow which his memory does not deserve. Wilson himself describes Lopez as "a Cuban adventurer," but he was blinded by his righteous indignation against slavery and the power that tried to enforce its continuation, to the point of committing an injustice against a man whose whole life is the best proof that his motives were pure and dictated by the most disinterested patriotism. A man who had thrown up such a position as Lopez had held in Spain in order to devote himself to the work which he undertook, can hardly be called an adventurer.

As to the intentions of those who helped him by furnishing him with the means of undertaking

SPANISH RULE IN CUBA.

his expeditions, they were probably—in many cases —the outcome of a sincere and honest desire of helping Cuba because her cause was just, and in other instances based, most likely, upon reasons not so generous. For it is unquestionable that here again the hydra of the slave power raised one of its many heads. The motives of many of those who furnished the filibustering expeditions of that time with arms, ammunition, etc. were as unworthy as those of the Southern Representatives who during the administration of John Quincy Adams had protested in Congress against the suppression of the Spanish domination in Cuba. From the administration of President Polk to the administration of President Buchanan, including the latter, the same policy in favor of the continuance of slavery prevailed which had influenced the actions of the government of this country from twenty to thirty-five years before, with this difference, that [1] "while under President Adams, Cuba had been an object of dread, it became at a later period an object of vehement desire."

---

[1] Henry Wilson, "Rise and Fall of the Slave Power in America," 2nd vol. page 610.

In 1846, an American Company had been formed for the purpose of purchasing Cuba for two hundred million dollars. In the same year fifteen hundred men commanded by Colonel White were on the verge of leaving for Cuba on a filibustering expedition, but were stopped by the American government. In 1848 Polk had authorized the American Minister at Madrid to offer one hundred million dollars for the island, but the offer had been at once rejected. In 1852, advances were made by England and France to the government of this country leading to a common action of the three governments in guaranteeing to Spain the possession of Cuba, but the proposition was declined. Among the reasons assigned by Mr. Everett, our Secretary of State, for that declination was one "in which slavery though not specifically mentioned was undoubtedly meant, and the apprehended danger thereto from the proposed arrangement was urged as one consideration why it should not be consummated." [1]

---

[1] Henry Wilson, "Rise and Fall of the Slave Power in America," 2nd vol, page 611.

SPANISH RULE IN CUBA.

The administrations of that time were strongly under the influence of Southern interests,[1] and evidently the story of the endeavors made during all that period to secure the release of Cuba from the Spanish rule does not constitute one of the glorious pages of American history; nevertheless whatever the intentions of the different administrations may have been, or of part of those who helped in various ways the expeditions undertaken at that time, there can be no doubt that much of the feeling manifested in favor of the Cubans by the people was due to a clean and genuine sense of sympathy for their sufferings and to a desire for their relief.

But if it is certain that the policy of the various administrations which have been referred to was directed towards the increase of the vote favorable to the maintenance of slavery through the acquisition of one or more slave states, it is by no means equally true that public opinion in the United States, or even within the Democratic party, was unanimous in favoring the annexation of Cuba, for even in the South the opinion was divided as to

---
(1) See note 4, page 203.

that annexation, or at least as to the time at which it might have become desirable.

I have before me the number for January, 1852, of the "Southern Quarterly Review," published in Charleston by W. Gilmore Sims. The editor begins by making a furious onslaught against Lopez and his companions, whom he calls "a small band of desperate adventurers." He says that they had deceived the public of this country, that the Cubans did not want to be separated from Spain, and that this was proved by the failure of the two expeditions. "To the States of the North," continues the editor, referring to the annexation, "the institution of slavery in Cuba would have occasioned new difficulties," while "to the people of our Southern States what motive could there be in bringing the State of Cuba under the control of a power from which we are almost prepared to shake ourselves free. * * * Surely it will be time enough to think of adding Cuba to our domain when we ourselves are rendered secure, no matter by what means, from the perpetual annoyance of abolition."

Further on he states that "Lopez was a monomaniac,"—this is the truth, since he was possessed of the same sublime mania which impelled the actions of Washington, Garibaldi and a few others; only he lacked the means of carrying his aberrations of mind to a successful issue—"And," adds the editor, "the passion for the liberation of Cuba from foreign (not from Spanish) rule was probably just tinctured with another passion *'not altogether apparent to himself'* by which the acquisition *'and the retention'* of Cuban liberty was to be enjoyed through his administration." The italics are mine; it is impossible to insinuate more gracefully an accusation to the support of which no proof can be brought. The editor tries to prove that Lopez was directed by a desire of personal domination over the Island, and only succeeds in showing that he had a noble ambition of being useful to his country. But the mainstay of the charges brought by the Review against Lopez was . . . . . Cuban bonds! Truly, there is nothing new under the sun.

Here we have a perfect illustration of the words of the famous Aria in Rossini's "Barber of Seville:"

" La calunnia è un venticello"

which may be translated as follows in English rhyme of the same value as that usually found in the translations of operatic librettos:

>Slander is a zephyr mild
>'Tis a very gentle breeze
>Which insensibly one day
>Murmurs, whispers, softly whispers,
>Thus insinuates its way.

And then it goes crescendo, until it bursts out "come un colpo di cannone," with the noise of a cannon shot—and no one knows how the rumor started.

On such flimsy charges the accusations against Lopez have been based.

In the midst of that lot of rubbish there is in the Review a statement which under an unpolished surface conceals a gem of truth. "There is," says the editor, "there is a third class among our people scattered over all the Southern States, but particularly active in the Northern, whose sympathies are forever at work in behalf of all the world's discon-

SPANISH RULE IN CUBA.

tents. They are those who believe with the impudent Frenchman who expressed the opinion that had he been consulted at the Creation he could have suggested a great many improvements in the plans of Providence."

The exaggeration here is evident, and the sarcasm would turn into a Quixotic sentiment, a most noble feeling of sympathy for the oppressed; but those words, coming from a source which cannot be suspected of favoring the plans of the annexationists, are of some value in demonstrating that the attitude of the United States at that time has been painted, for party reasons, in blacker colors than it really deserved, and that the agitation was not entirely due to the furtherance of the cause of slavery, for there was a "third class"—and it was a large one—which was prompted by more worthy motives.

Nevertheless it cannot be doubted that, in the main, what the party then in power was seeking was a political balance against the increase of free States, and the addition of the white population of Cuba to the Democratic vote.

The Democratic National Conventions of 1856 and 1860 expressed themselves as being "in favor of the acquisition of Cuba," and their motive was hardly disguised. The administration of Mr. Buchanan made energetical efforts in that direction. In 1858 the President complained, in his annual message, of the unsatisfactory condition of the relations of the country with Spain.[1] Referring to the participation of Cuba in the African slave trade he affirmed his belief that the last relic of that traffic would disappear if Cuba were annexed. A bill was introduced in the Senate shortly after, placing thirty million dollars in the hands of the President towards the purchase of the Island, and was favorably reported on by the Committee on Foreign Affairs, but the matter did not come to an issue.

If the philanthropy of the motives of President Buchanan is extremely questionable, there can on the other hand be no difficulty in understanding or interpreting the words which Senator Brown spoke soon after the adjournment of Congress. "Cuba

---

[1] Henry Wilson, "Rise and Fall of the Slave Power in America," 2nd vol. page 612.

SPANISH RULE IN CUBA.

must and shall be ours," said the Senator in a speech in New York.⁽¹⁾ " * * * It may be asked, what do we want of Cuba? We want it for territorial expansion, we want it to extend our commerce. Then I have a little reason of my own. I want Cuba for the extension of slavery. I have freely spoken the sentiments of my own heart and of a vast majority of the Democracy throughout the Union. The Democratic party is going into the next Presidential canvass upon this and other questions, and we intend to meet Seward face to face upon it."

We have, however, to go back to the Administration of President Pierce in order to find the most interesting episodes in the relations of that period between the United States and Spain in regard to the Cuban question.

On the 3d of March, 1855, President Pierce transmitted to the House of Representatives the correspondence between Secretary Marcy and Ministers Soule and Buchanan, who represented the United

---

(1) Henry Wilson, "Rise and Fall of the Slave Power in America," 2nd vol. page 612.

States, respectively, at the Courts of Madrid and Paris. This correspondence showed that on July 23d, 1853, Mr. Marcy had written to Soule that the Island of Cuba was very difficult for Spain to retain "in its present state of dependence," and that it was "confidently believed" that she could not "long sustain, unaided, her present connection with the Island." The United States, stated the Secretary, would resist at all hazards the transference of Cuba to any other European nation, but while Spain remained "in fact as well as in name" the sovereign of Cuba she could depend upon our "maintaining our duty as a neutral nation towards her, however difficult it might be." Our government could not be suspected of conniving at the participation of our citizens in past disturbances in the Island. It was insisted that neutrality laws had been observed "and could not be made more restrictive without violating the Constitutional rights of our citizens." The offer of purchase made under President Polk was referred to, and it was stated that, however, there had been no intention of pur-

SPANISH RULE IN CUBA.

chasing the Island "unless its inhabitants were very generally disposed to concur in the transfer." Mr. Soule was directed to find out what arrangements had been made by Spain with Great Britain and France in regard to sustaining her dominion over Cuba, and how far they, or either of them, were urging a change in the internal condition of the Island, "particularly in regard to the slaves now there or to the present system of labor." Another offer of purchase was not advised, as it was not believed that Spain would accept it. The belief was expressed that Spain was under obligations to Great Britain and France not to transfer the Island to the United States, and it was thought that Spain would "pertinaciously hold on to Cuba and that the separation, whenever it will take place, will be the work of violence." The suggestion was made that "Spain might in a manner consistent with her national honor and advantageous to her interests * * * give birth to an independent nation of her own race, retaining at the same time a commercial intercourse with it as profitable as she can have in a connection prolonged by force." "Our flag," wrote Mr. Marcy, "must be respected and our commerce relieved from embarrassment by the Cuban authorities. The United States will not submit to have their merchant vessels searched or detained in their lawful voyages." Complaints in this regard, said the Secretary, had never received attention.

In February, 1854, an event occurred which, though now almost forgotten, caused great excitement in this country at that time and came near putting an end to the apparent friendly relations between the United States and Spain.

The steamer Black Warrior, a packet-ship of the New York and Alabama Line, commanded by Captain Bullock, plying between Mobile and New York and calling on every trip at Havana, was seized under a futile pretense, and in defiance of all precedents, by the authorities in the latter port. The Black Warrior came from Mobile and had on board a cargo of 900 bales of cotton, destined to New York. It had been the habit both of the Black Warrior and of other vessels engaged in the

SPANISH RULE IN CUBA. 87

same traffic, when calling at Havana in transit without unloading any portion of the cargo, to enter the vessel as being in ballast. This, Captain Bullock had done on thirty-six previous occasions, and the steamers of other lines had done it over three hundred times; although the proceeding was irregular, no objection had ever been made by the Spanish authorities, but on this particular trip the vessel was seized and a fine of $6,000 imposed on Captain Bullock. He hauled down the flag and left the Spanish authorities in possession of the vessel. Captain Watson, of the United States Steamer Fulton, who was then in port, on hearing of the outrage, intended to haul his vessel alongside the Black Warrior, drive out the Spaniards and take her out of the harbor, but finally our Consul, and Captain Bullock himself, prevailed on him to desist from his purpose.

A protest was sent by the American citizens residing at Havana to Secretary Marcy, and the latter in directing Minister Soule, on March 11, 1854, to call the attention of the government of

Spain to the seizure, complained of the dilatory tactics of that country in other matters of the same kind which had been the subject of previous correspondence. In another letter, dated March 17, the Secretary instructed Soule to demand a sum of $300,000 as compensation to the owners of the Black Warrior and of the cargo, stating that the course of Spain had usually been an evasion of our claims but that it would not do in this case. The President in his message to Congress of March 15th, transmitted the report of the Secretary complaining of aggression upon our commerce, violation of our rights and insults to the national flag by the Spanish authorities in Cuba.

Soule presented the claim on the 11th of April, and pressed it forcibly in several letters; finally he obtained an answer in which the Spanish Minister of State asked for more time, and complained of the "harsh and imperious" expressions of the American Minister. Soule answered that the records of the Legation were loaded with reclamations bearing on grievances most flagrant, which had never been

SPANISH RULE IN CUBA.

attended to, and were met with just such dilatory excuses, and he added: "If there be cases in which it may become a great nation to show itself magnanimous, even under the infliction of most unwarrantable injuries, it can never be when such injuries are coupled with so barefaced a disregard of what is due to a friendly power, as that which was exhibited towards the United States in the detention of the Black Warrior, and in the confiscation of her cargo." The correspondence was continued between Soule and Spanish Minister Calderon de la Barca, in the same bitter tones and with the same unsatisfactory results. In a letter dated April 20th, Soule referred to no less than twelve grievances and claims for seizures, detentions and other acts against American citizens, stating that these cases were only a few of those appearing in the archives of the Legation.

On the 3d of April, Marcy wrote to Soule that the President gave him full power to enter a convention or treaty for the purchase of Cuba, stating distinctly, however, that "in any conceivable arrangements of this kind the people of Cuba must necessarily be a party to them." Soule in writing to the Secretary on the 3d of May advised that a lesson be given to Spain.

On the 16th of August of the same year, Secretary Marcy wrote to Soule that he was directed by the President to suggest to him "a particular step from which he anticipates much advantage in the negotiations on the subject of Cuba." Further details as to this particular step were withheld from Congress, and do not appear in the correspondence as transmitted by President Pierce. "Much may be done," added Mr. Marcy, "at London and Paris to promote directly the object in view, or to clear away impediments to its successful consummation," and he advises him to meet Buchanan and Mason (the latter being Minister to London), suggesting that a conference be held at Paris.

The conference between the three ministers was held at Ostend in October, 1854, and gave rise to the famous document known as the Ostend mani-

SPANISH RULE IN CUBA.   91

fest. This lengthy and extraordinary paper stated, in substance, that Cuba should be obtained from Spain peaceably by purchase, if possible, but by force of arms if necessary, and if its suggestions had been adopted the United States would have entered into a war of conquest, entirely against the nature of our principles and institutions. The truculent spirit of the manifest was probably due to the influence of Soule, who was impatient of restraint and was urging the Administration not to delay the solution and to take advantage of the Crimean war in which all the strength and energies of the European powers were then engaged in order to wage war against Spain without fear of European interference; he afterwards resigned from his post because his suggestions were not carried out.

Fortunately, however, for the honor of the United States, Soule's policy was not adopted; Mr. Marcy wrote to him, under date of November 13, 1854, that if the "cession of Cuba" had "to be hopelessly abandoned for the present" the United States would still ask "and pertinaciously insist upon some security against the further misconduct of the Spanish authorities at Cuba;" but the claim in regard to the Black Warrior was finally allowed to drop, the vessel having been released on the payment of the fine of $6,000 which had been imposed on the Captain; Spain through her dilatory tactics had fully succeeded in her purpose of evading our demands.

Thus, from what precedes may be seen that while the party then in power in this country was largely influenced in its conduct towards Spain by the partisans of the system of slavery, it is not correct to say that the filibustering expeditions of that time were distinctly to provide for the maintenance and extension of that system, for there was undoubtedly among the people a strong sense of sympathy for the Cubans on account of the wrongs which they were suffering, and the United States had beyond question many just causes of complaint against Spain for the manner in which she interfered with our commerce and disregarded the respect due to our flag.

SPANISH RULE IN CUBA.

Let us revert to the maxim which has been so justly and correctly set forth by Molmenti.

Can it be thought that had any European nation been in the same position towards Spain in which the United States were at that time it would have resisted the pressure exerted by the dominant power in its politics, and refrained from attacking a weaker nation which would have been hopelessly alone in the contest? Any one of the claims which the United States had against Spain might have furnished a better pretense for a war than the reason, for instance, for which France and Germany went to war in 1870. But the policy of the United States, whatever may have been the unworthy influences which sought to direct it in a wrong channel, was and has always been honorable and above board. It was not found possible to acquire Cuba by a purchase, and with the consent of the people of the Island, therefore the matter was dropped; no war of conquest was undertaken.

The spirit of the nation had triumphed over the spirit of a party; it is for this reason, because above the party cliques, the rings and the unavowable schemes towers the genius of the Constitution that the principles of the fathers of this Republic will forever guide it in the path of virtue, of right and of progress; and we may hopefully believe that, notwithstanding present appearances to the contrary, it will yet be this nation which will logically and peacefully point the way to those social reforms which have become as necessary to our civilization as political liberties were to our elders, and are still to us.

Every American citizen is not a saint. It is easy enough for some men after a short stay in this country to scatter broadcast their hastily gathered and mistaken impressions, or for others who would abolish the sun because it is darkened by a few spots to rake up all the undesirable elements of American politics, but the liberal minded man who studies the history of this country cannot fail to admire this great nation. The slanderers forget that for every one of them, to whatever nationality he may belong, there are one hundred thousand or more of his countrymen who have made this country their home, and who with few exceptions, whatever may have been their personal success in life, have become sufficiently attached to it to adopt it as their own.

CHAPTER IX.

The Ten Years' War in Cuba—Proclamation of Independence—General Dulce and the Volunteers—The Orders of Balmaseda—The Battle of La Sacra—A Reign of Terror—Pacification of the Island by General Martinez Campos—The Treaty of El Zanjon and How Spain Observed Its Provisions.

While the events which have been related in the preceding chapter were taking place several governors had succeeded each other in the administration of Cuba. In 1854 the Cuban Junta in New York had made preparations for an expedition; Captain-General Jose de la Concha threatened to Africanize the Island; he armed the negroes and the Peninsulars, and disarmed the white native Cubans. A conspiration was discovered; two patriots, Pinto and Estrampes were garroted, and one hundred others were sent to prisons in Spain. The proposed expedition was given up, and de la Concha was created Marquis of Havana as a reward for his services. General Serrano, who succeeded Concha, and after him General Dulce, were inclined to a policy of conciliation with the Cubans, but were strongly opposed by the Ultra-Conservative Spanish party of the Island. The treasury had been considerably depleted by Concha's dishonesty, and economical conditions went from bad to worse, till in 1866 the deficit was enormous. Lersundi, who succeeded Dulce, was a governor after the heart of the Conservatives; he reestablished the Military Commissions, as had existed in Tacon's time, and the vexations and oppressions of these Commissions, together with the imposition of still heavier taxes increased the dissatisfaction among the native population. Scandalous frauds were being committed by the officials in charge of the collection of taxes. Undoubtedly the execution of Maximilian in Mexico served to encourage the hopes of the Cuban patriots, as it testified to the decline of European influence in America. At about that time, and in the middle of all these troubles a bitter quarrel between the Captain-General and the Bishop of Havana occurred, and increased the disorder among the Conservatives; it arose from the grave and important question of whether the bells of the churches should ring at the entrance of the Captain General into a city, as a mark of respect, which the representative of the military authority claimed was due him.

The debt of the Island in 1868 was about 400,000,000 Reales;[1] the deficit reached nearly 355,000,000, and still the government was drawing to the amount of 50,000,000 Reales yearly against the resources of the Island, while the people were groaning under the weight of the taxes which were imposed solely for the benefit of the mother country. The crimes and errors of Spain had reached a culminating point, and were to result in the long and bloody civil war which followed.

On the 18th of November, 1868, an outbreak occurred among the negroes in Porto Rico, at the cry of "Viva la libertad!" and with the object of gaining independence from Spain. The Cuban liberals who had in vain been striving to obtain administrative reforms, the freedom of the press, the assimilation of Cubans to the Spaniards in regard

---

[1] A real is worth five cents or a little less.

SPANISH RULE IN CUBA.

to political and civil rights, the right of assembly, the reduction of taxation, etc., broke out into open hostilities on hearing the news. The insurrection still lacked a leader, but this was soon found in the person of Carlos Emanuel Cespedes.

Cespedes was born at Bayamo in 1819; he graduated from the University of Havana and subsequently went to Spain and obtained the degree of "Licenciado" of the law (Doctor of law) from the University of Barcelona, in 1842; while in that country he became friendly with General Prim and took part in the attempt of the latter at establishing a Republican form of government, but the attempt having failed he was banished, and went to France. Thence, in 1844, he returned to Cuba where he practiced law in his native town of Bayamo. He had always been devoted to the cause of his native Island and in 1852 he was arrested and held for five months in Morro Castle because he had, at a banquet, spoken words in favor of the liberation of Cuba from the Spanish rule.

On the 10th of October, 1868, Cespedes pro-

FOUR CENTURIES OF

Carlos Manuel Cespedes.

Captain-General Caballero De Rodas.   Antonio Maceo.

claimed from a sugar plantation in the neighborhood of Yara, the independence of the Island. He issued a manifest, in which the oppressive Spanish rule, the immorality of the functionaries, the excessive taxes arbitrarily collected, and other evils were bitterly complained of, and he announced the principles of the secessionists to be the gradual emancipation of the slaves through indemnization to the owners, equal rights for all, respect to life and property, universal suffrage, and free trade. On issuing this proclamation he affirmed his sincerity by granting absolute and unconditional liberty to his own slaves. Subsequently, during the course of the Revolution, Cespedes was killed by the Spaniards on the 27th of February, 1874, having been betrayed by a negro who revealed the hiding place of his chief in order to save his own life.

From Yara, the insurrection spread into the other provinces, and the insurgents took possession of Bayamo, and successively of Camaguey, without meeting serious opposition. A mixed Committee composed of both Spaniards and Cubans begged

Governor Lersundi to inaugurate a policy of reform, and only succeeded in being treated as rebels. Bodies of Volunteers were organized, composed of men who were virtually aliens in Cuba, as they belonged entirely to the Peninsular class, and these organizations became responsible for a large share of the outrages which were committed by the Spaniards during the course of that war which was to last no less than ten years.

Finally the Madrid Government recalled Lersundi, and superseded him by General Dulce who was somewhat more liberally inclined, and offered certain administrative reforms; but the offer came too late and was refused by the insurgents who had gained possession of a large portion of the Island, and encouraged by their success refused to treat unless on a basis of absolute independence. Dulce was also hampered in his efforts at conciliation by the Volunteers who now constituted an armed and ferocious mob, committing numerous acts of cruelty and absolute murder, and who for a long time held full sway over the Island in defiance alike of the government of Spain and of the Insular Cubans.

General Balmaseda, after several encounters of small importance with the insurgents, marched on Bayamo which was abandoned by the Cubans, but not before they had completely destroyed it. Their number continued to increase; Dulce now called new reinforcements from Spain and changed his policy to one of severe repression. Still this was not sufficient to please the Conservatives, or as they were called the "Unconditionals," the party among which the Volunteers were recruited. Even his orders that all property belonging to the insurgents should be seized failed to satisfy them, and they became so powerful and so desperate in their greed for the blood of the Insulars, which Dulce, however severe, did not shed in quantities sufficient to appease their wrath, that they finally drove the governor away from the Island, in June, 1870. There were at that time 110,000 Spanish soldiers in Cuba.

The Madrid government sent General Caballero de Rodas to take Dulce's place.

A house of Representatives of the Cuban Republic, consisting of fifteen men had met at Guaimaro, and voted a constitution. Cespedes, in succession of Cisneros whom the Cubans had at first placed at the head of the Civil Government, was elected President, and Manuel Quesada named Commander-in-Chief. The latter's place was afterwards taken by Thomas Jordan, an American, a graduate of West Point, and ex-Confederate officer. It may be interesting to note that General Jordan, on his return to the United States, stated that with a nucleus of hardy and disciplined American soldiers he could gather an efficient army, which, properly armed, would drive the Spaniards into the sea in ninety days.

The war continued with varied success; at one time fortune having of late been unfavorable to the insurrection, de Rodas thought that he had suppressed it, and returned to Spain. General Balmaseda was then given full command of the army, and this time the Volunteers had indeed found a man who was ready to give them complete satisfaction, for it was Balmaseda, who already since the 4th of April, 1869, had issued the famous proclamation that every male over fifteen years of age found in the country away from his home without plausible reason should be shot, every house on which a white flag was not displayed should be burnt, and all women and children found alone on their farms should be removed by force to Bayamo or Jiguany. The Cubans retaliated in kind, and no quarter was given on either side.

The mistake made by De Rodas was soon found out for the insurgents kept up a persistent guerrilla warfare, headed by Agramonte, Maximo Gomez, Sanguilly, Garcia, Maceo and others, until in 1873 they had regained all the territory which had been previously lost by them. In November of that year a real battle was fought at La Sacra, resulting in the defeat of the Spanish troops. Shortly after Maximo Gomez having routed a Spanish force composed of a thousand cavalry, eight battalions of infantry and several pieces of artillery advanced under Puerto Principe, and the cause of the insurgents gained thereby considerable credit and advantage.

In 1874 General Jovellar whom the Spanish Republic had sent as Captain General continued the reign of terror of his predecessors. All men between twenty and forty-five years of age were forced into the militia, also one-tenth of those over forty-five, and one slave out of every thousand was claimed for military labor. The Volunteers declared that the vigorous system would crush the Revolution in six months, while the insurgents felt equally sure and insisted that they would capture Puerto Principe in six days; both were in error. At different times, a number of Spanish soldiers deserted to the Cuban forces, and their fate whenever they happened to be captured was not doubtful. In 1875 the Captain General concentrated all the troops which he disposed against Gomez and defeated him in several encounters.

In order to meet the deficient budget and to provide for the exigencies of the war the Authorities of Havana had, in October 1872, made a large increase of taxation. Every slave hired out had been taxed $24; the export duties and the war tax on Real Estate had been doubled, and the war tax on bankers and merchants, as well as the war tax on imported goods increased from ten to twenty-five per cent. In 1876 the Spanish government concluded a convention with Spanish Capitalists for an advance of five million dollars.

General Martinez Campos was sent from Spain to take part in the operations in Cuba as Commander-in-Chief of the Army, in October, 1876. Later Jovellar was recalled and Martinez Campos placed in supreme military and civil command.

Since 1877, the fortunes of the Insurgents had declined. Martinez Campos who, it is said, had been privately instructed by King Alfonso to make peace on any terms, adopted a more conciliatory policy towards the insurgents. He held out promises of reform and of improvement in the economical and political conditions of the Island. Several influential chiefs surrendered; finally Gomez himself laid down his arms, and peace was restored by the treaty of El Zanjon, in 1878. In August of that year, however, a new revolt broke out, as soon as the number of the Spanish troops had been decreased. As it was confined entirely to the colored population, and the whites held apart, it was soon defeated.

The Spanish promises proved illusory. Constitutional reform was the base on which the insurgents had capitulated, and in fact Cuba was authorized to send Deputies to the Cortes, and Provincial Assemblies were provided for, but the system of election and the regulations which were subsequently promulgated by the Spanish government in that connection were such that, in substance, the Governor General still retained full power in his own hands. The Deputies to the Cortes could accomplish nothing, and Spain continued to control absolutely and for her own advantage, without regard for the interests or desires of the Cubans, the tariff, the taxes and in general the mode of raising and expending the revenue of the Island. The abolition of slavery was completed in 1886, but the political and economical difficulties continued. As usual, Spain had not profited by her own experience or by that of other colonizing nations, and continued the same policy of injustice and spoliation towards the Cubans.

CHAPTER X.

The Ten Years' War in the United States—The Sentiment in 1868—Cuban War News in 1869—The Wishes of General Grant—Resolutions That Were Not Adopted — The Filibustering Expeditions — The Brigs "Mary Lowell," and the "Lizzie Major"— The Promises of Spain – The "Virginius" Affair—How Spain Abused the Patience and Forbearance of the United States.

The beginning of the ten years' war had found the general condition of things in the United States very different from what it had been at the time of the expeditions of Lopez and during the period which immediately followed it. An internal strife of great length and severity had taken place; the government of the country had passed into the hands of another party; slavery had been eliminated from our social system and the sympathy which the people of the American Union continued to feel, and manifested more clearly than ever, for the cause of Cuban liberty had been considerably purified from suspicious motives and influences. The general sentiment in this country when Cespedes took the field was that Cuba should be delivered from all Spanish dominion; as to what was to become of it after it was freed, the sentiment was divided. It was held by some that it should be given existence as an independent state, and by others that it should be annexed to this country. The Editor of "Harper's Weekly" said, in the number for April 10th, 1869, of that periodical, that there were at that time two Cuban parties in this country; "one wishing that Cuba might get its liberty, the other that we might get Cuban sugar. One, the party of Cuban independence, the other, of Cuban annexation;" but it should be remembered that that magazine was then and has been ever since, and even recently, persistently opposed to the annexation of Cuba to the United States, and although it has time and again felt compelled to protest vigorously against the outrages which were being committed in the Island, it has always insisted on our maintaining a strict neutrality in the contest.

New York was then, as well as recently, the headquarters of the Cuban patriots, most of those who emigrated from Cuba since 1850 having sought refuge in this country. In fact the emigration to New York disturbed the authorities of Cuba to such an extent that, in 1869, they spread the rumor that New York was infested with small-pox in order to discourage further travel to that city. The reports which reached here from the seat of the revolution were often very puzzling to the public mind. The same periodical quoted above said, under date of May 15th, 1869: "The situation in Cuba at the present moment is one which it is almost impossible to comprehend. On the one side, taking the Cuban accounts, it would appear that the enthusiasm of the rebels was never greater than it is now; while the Spanish statements which we read make the cause of the insurgents seem absolutely hopeless." These words have a strangely familiar sound to our ears, for they describe the same discrepancies in the news of the fight to which we have been accustomed during the present Cuban Revolution, and which Mr. Halstead with an extremely happy expression has called "an irrepressible conflict of testimony."

Among the wild rumors which were set afloat in the United States for partisan reasons during the course of the ten years' war, was one to the effect that this country was to go to war against Spain in the interests of a third term for President Grant, for such a war would have been extremely popular and would have increased the vote in his favor.

General Grant was really very much inclined to favor the aspirations of the Cubans, but certainly not for the nonsensical reason which was for a moment absurdly given in explanation of his views. He shared the traditions of the army, and as soon as the revolution broke out at Yara he wished to acknowledge the belligerency of the Insurgents and recognize the independence of the Island. General Rawlings, the Secretary of War, encouraged him in that direction, but he was opposed by Mr. Fish, then Secretary of State, and the influence of the latter finally prevailed in shaping the course of the President's policy, although his sympathies were not affected by it, for in 1875 Secretary Fish wrote to Mr. Cushing, American Minister at Madrid, that the President regarded "independence and emancipation as the only certain and even necessary solution of the Cuban question." In a message, in 1870, President Grant stated that he had made representations to the Spanish government "for securing to the people of Cuba the blessings and the right of self-government." Again, in another message, in 1876, he said that there was "no good reason either for acknowledging the independence of the insurgents or their belligerency," but he added that the interests of the United States and of humanity demanded the cessation of the strife. When Balmaseda issued his famous edict, Secretary Fish, in a letter to the American Minister at Madrid, protested against "the infamous order of General, the Count of Balmaseda."

Resolutions were many times introduced in Congress in favor of the insurgents. In June, 1870, General Banks and General Logan, in ardent appeals in behalf of the recognition of the Cubans as belligerents, declared that we were guilty of their slaughter and of the sacrifice of liberty in America if we did not interfere. General Banks said that the prayers of the people of this country for the success of the ·Cubans were well nigh universal. Mr. Sumner also offered resolutions declaring "the sympathy of the people of the United States with their fellow-Americans in Cuba," and deploring the ferocity of Cuban warfare on both sides. Mr. Cox, of New York, in January, 1872, introduced in the House of Representatives a resolution recognizing the independence of the Island, in consequence of eight students at Havana having been shot for a mere boyish freak; again, on December 27, 1873, he offered a resolution acknowledging the belligerency of the revolutionists, but the House refused to consider it by a vote of 153 to 44. In fact all such resolutions always failed to pass either one or the other branch of Congress, or both, and very properly, since the independence of a country and the belligerency of those who endeavor to establish it are not to be acknowledged by other countries merely because it is a matter of right; the power to enforce that right

SPANISH RULE IN CUBA. 115

must be shown, and the possession of an organization capable, not only nominally but in reality, of conducting effectively all the civil functions of a government must be proved to complete satisfaction. This the Cuban insurgents never could do, and consequently, notwithstanding our desire of helping their cause, their belligerency and the independence of the Island were never acknowledged.

In the year 1873, an event occurred which because of the interest which it excited in this country and of the results which it threatened to have deserves to be related at some length.

The government of this country having decided to remain neutral in the contest between Spain and her Colony made then, as it had during a previous period, and has since during the present revolution, all the efforts in its power to enforce the laws of neutrality, and these efforts were loyally and sincerely made, although Spain has never been capable of appreciating such loyalty and sincerity[1] and of understanding that any further action would have been contrary to the rights which the citizens of this

---
[1] See note 5, page 203.

country enjoy under its Constitution. However, it could not be expected—it was against the nature of things—that the American citizen, born to liberty and possessing an innate feeling of revolt against anything that may savor of political oppression, should view with indifference the unfair, unequal struggle which was taking place at the very doors of his land between a few thousand hungry and ragged men trying to secure their own rights and a nation possessing the resources, the wealth and the trained and well-armed forces of which Spain then disposed. The result was that notwithstanding the vigilance which the Administration exerted during the periods of all the different Cuban revolutions, it always found it impossible to prevent some of the citizens of this Union from giving now and then in their private capacity a substantial proof of their friendship for the Cuban rebels by furnishing them with recruits as well as with articles of clothing, food, arms, ammunition, etc. Besides, the Cuban refugees in this country were naturally active, as they had been in Lopez' time, and as they have been

SPANISH RULE IN CUBA.

recently, in organizing such assistance in the shape of filibustering expeditions.

Many vessels were occasionally engaged in secretly taking men and merchandise to appropriate spots on the Cuban coast and had been the source of much trouble between the United States and Spain, on account of the arbitrary action of the Spanish authorities. In 1869, the "Mary Lowell," an American brig loaded with arms put into a port in the Bahamas and while there was seized by a Spanish man-of-war and taken to Havana, in spite of the protests of the British authorities in that port who were, at that time, unable to enforce such protests and prevent the outrage. Again, on another occasion, passengers were taken from an American vessel, the brig "Lizzie Major," and imprisoned. Secretary Fish told the Spanish Minister in Washington that the prisoners should be released and an apology and indemnity and ample reparation of every kind offered, and the Minister answered that Spain would undoubtedly give satisfaction. There was some delay in hearing from the Spanish government; Mr. Fish having sent again for the Minister, suggested to him that such delay was very dangerous, and it was only on being almost forced to the wall that Spain acceded to our demands. General Dulce had issued a proclamation that all vessels with arms and ammunition on board should be treated as pirates; Mr. Fish told the Spanish Minister that this order was a violation of recognized international right, and upon representations to Madrid the Spanish government disavowed the proclamation, but how sincere and effective was that disavowal will soon be seen.

In October, 1873, the "Virginius," a little, wooden, side-wheeled steamer, with a crew of fifty-two men sailed from Kingston, Jamaica, bound for Lemon Bay. Twelve of the crew were of American citizenship, the others being subjects of England and of other countries. Captain Joseph Fry, who was in command of the vessel, was a son of Major Fry of the United States Army, who died in Florida during the Seminole Indian war; he had graduated as a passed midshipman from the school at

SPANISH RULE IN CUBA.

Annapolis in 1842. In 1847 he had fought a duel with Midshipman Brown of Mississippi, but after drawing his antagonist's fire he had generously refused to return it. He had served for many years before the war, and when Louisiana seceded he had thrown up his lieutenant's commission and entered the Confederate Army. The record of his whole life was good.

The owner of the Virginius was Joseph W. Patterson of New Orleans, who is said to have been an agent of the Cuban insurgents, and had been able to obtain papers for his vessel from that port. Besides the crew, the vessel carried 113 passengers, many but not all of whom were citizens of this country, and it was stated on good authority that many of them were bound on a business or pleasure trip and were entirely ignorant of the fact that the Virginius was or had been engaged in carrying arms and ammunition to the revolutionists in Cuba. While the vessel was on the high seas, on the 1st of November, it was seized by the Spanish gunboat Tornado, and taken to Santiago. It is interesting to note that both the Virginius and the Tornado had been built by the same firm of ship builders for blockade runners, but the Tornado proved much the better boat at the time of the capture, for the hull and machinery of the Virginius were extremely dirty and in otherwise poor condition. The action of the Spanish authorities was in many ways illegal, one of the reasons for which it was unwarranted by international laws being that the seizure was executed outside of the three mile from shore limit prescribed in such cases. It took four days for the Tornado to bring its prize into the harbor of Santiago and the distance at which the Virginius was from the Cuban coast when it was captured may be guessed from this; but the Spanish authorities entirely disregarded the fact that in time of peace a vessel of any nation is subject, on the high seas, only to the police jurisdiction of the power from which it receives its papers. It is not denied that the Virginius had arms on board; but none were found on it at the time that she was captured as they had been thrown overboard when the cruiser had been sighted.

SPANISH RULE IN CUBA. 121

On November 4th, as soon as both vessels had arrived at Santiago, the prisoners were given the mockery of a trial before a drum head court martial. All treaty obligations, all regulations were set aside and ignored; there was no evidence against the prisoners, still they were all found guilty and sentenced to death.

This did not happen under a Monarch or a crowned despot, it happened under a Republic, for the Captain General then represented in Cuba the Spanish Republic of which Emilio Castelar became President. It was rumored that the execution had been countermanded, and the Volunteers declared in their organ, published in Havana, that "the Captain General would not dare to issue such an absurd order as an arrest of the Santiago executions."

On the same day on which that travesty on a trial had taken place, the day on which the Tornado and Virginius had arrived at Santiago, the 4th of November, those of the prisoners who were of Cuban birth, and one of the Americans, were killed. General Burriel, who directed the proceedings, in a letter of that date to the Captain General informed him that the persons whom he named in the letter had been shot "for being traitors to their country, and for being insurgent chiefs."

On the 7th of the same month, the Captain and crew of the Virginius were taken to the shooting-place, which was very appropriately named "the slaughter-house," and they were shot. Fry before the execution wrote a letter to his wife, a most touching and pathetic document, in which he said "There is to be a fearful sacrifice of life on the Virginius, and as I think, a needless one, as the poor people are unconscious of crime, and even of their fate up to now. I hope God will forgive me if I am to blame for it." It has been said that some of the crew of the Virginius had been forced on board against their will. Fifty-three men were killed in all in the two executions. Fry was magnanimously given the privilege of walking down the lines of his companions and bidding them adieu, before he was himself shot.

There still remained under sentence of death

Execution of the Crew of the Virginius.

ninety-three men belonging to the passenger list of the Virginius, but at this juncture matters took an unexpected and unwelcome turn for the Spaniards. Commodore de Horsey, in charge of the British Navy in the West Indies, was at Port Royal, and on hearing of the outrage he immediately dispatched the "Niobe," a British steamer then at Jamaica, under the command of Captain Sir Lampton Lorraine to Santiago. The Niobe started at full speed and on arriving in that harbor the Captain, who was landed even before his ship was anchored, demanded that the wholesale assassination which was taking place should be stopped, and his firmness and energy prevented the accomplishment of the other murders which had been contemplated. The American warship "Wyoming" soon after steamed into Santiago, and later the "Juniata," and the guns of both the English and the American vessels inspired the Spanish with such respect that they desisted from their purpose.

On hearing of the executions, Secretary Fish cabled to General Sickles, American Minister at

Madrid, to protest "in the name of this government and of civilization and humanity against the act as brutal, barbarous and an outrage upon the age," and to ask for ample reparation. Sickles, in acknowledging receipt of the cablegram, stated that having presented the protest to the Spanish minister of state the latter had rejected it by an ill-tempered note saying that "Spain would nevertheless consider and decide questions according to law and her dignity." Afterwards the Spanish Minister claimed that as soon as he had received the news from Cuba he had cabled to stop the executions, but we have seen the real reason which caused their discontinuance. On November 23d, General Sickles was on the verge of closing the Legation and leaving the property in charge of the Italian Minister, but the Spanish diplomats succeeded in quieting matters. The Virginius and the surviving passengers were turned over to the United States, but the correspondence in regard to the reparation dragged on for years. Spain accused the vessel of being a pirate, claiming that her papers were fraudulent, and her American nationality not established; President Grant stated in a message to Congress, in January 1874, that if her papers were irregular the Virginius had committed an offense against the United States, who alone had the right to interfere and to punish. Finally a settlement was made by which Spain agreed to give a salute to our flag unless she could prove to our satisfaction that the American flag was improperly borne by the Virginius; this had all along been the contention of Spain, but our answer to it was that even if such were the case and admitting that the American papers of the Virginius were fraudulent, the only authority competent to judge of the validity of such papers was the one from which they claimed to emanate. General Sickles stated that the Spanish government had agreed to accept a declaration made by him as proof of the American nationality of the vessel. Nevertheless the salute to the American flag was not given, although Spain could never satisfy us of the truth of her version, and she got out of the difficulty by the payment of a paltry sum of $80,000 to the heirs of the victims, which had been agreed upon. She promised to prosecute Burriel, but never did it.[1] Mr. Cox, of New York, declared in the House of Representatives that Congress was "pusillanimous and without the courage to kill a mouse, and that the diplomacy of the government had draggled the flag of the country in the dust," but he was rebuked by Mr. Beck of Kentucky and by General Hawley who sustained the Administration. The greatest excitement prevailed among the people against Secretary Fish, and meetings against him were held in New York.

Thus, Spanish diplomacy had obtained another triumph over the patience and forbearance of the United States, but if the case of the Black Warrior had been forgotten, the murder of the crew of the Virginius left in the ashes of the past some smoldering embers, which Spain might eventually find exceedingly dangerous to fan into new life.

---

[1] As late as the 23d of April 1877, it was said in the British House of Commons that Spain had promised to try General Burriel, of the Virginius massacre notoriety, but that the trial had been delayed "on account of the non-receipt of papers from Cuba."

CHAPTER XI.

The Ten Years' War in Spain — Hopes That Were in Vain — King Amadeus, His Influence and His Abdication — A Modern Cicero — Emilio Castelar and the Genius of Spain.

When the government of Isabella had been upset, the hope was manifested in this country that while the old Spanish rule had been tyrannical, since it had been thrown off Spain, the new rule would prove less harsh. It was confidently expected that the humane and generous spirit which Castelar was supposed to represent would not continue to oppress the Cubans, or prolong the ferocities of past Spanish warfare.

Subsequent events, however, have given plentiful evidence that Spanish governments may come and go but the tyranny in Cuba will go on forever—until it is stopped by an iron hand.

The only faint ray of light in the Spanish political sky appeared during the reign of King Amadeus. Had he been able to bring Spanish public opinion to his own views, which were the outcome of a differ-

SPANISH RULE IN CUBA. 129

Spanish Guerrilla, Protecting the Passage of a Military Convoy.

ent way of thinking, befitting the people and the family to which he belonged, in that case most likely the situation of the Cubans would have improved; but he could not do it; it would have required a reformation of the whole Spanish character. After a short trial, during the course of which he came near losing his life, he gave up the job and the throne in indignation and disgust. The son of Victor Emanuel, of a man possessed of an honesty and a good, sound common sense rarely to be found in a king,[1] himself a member of a nation which is such a leader in civilization that a few years later it was to strike out the death penalty from its statute-books, Amadeus perforce felt out of place amid such surroundings.

It was, however, through his influence that the only genuine reform that Spain ever granted Cuba was effected. A code of rules enforcing the abolition of slavery in Cuba and Porto Rico was published by a decree of King Amadeus in 1872. The Cortes had indeed passed as early as 1869 an ordinance making preparations for the emancipation of

---

[1] See note 6, page 203.

the slaves in the Spanish Colonies, but it may safely be asserted that had it not been for the pressure exerted by that Italian the good measure would have gone the way of all other Spanish promises of reform, that is, it would have fallen into "innocuous desuetude." For the second time in her history Spain had become indebted to Italy.

It must be acknowledged that Amadeus was ably seconded in his efforts in that direction by Emilio Castelar.

In a speech in the Cortes, before the abdication of Amadeus, on the abolition of slavery in Cuba and Porto Rico, Castelar insisted on the "indissolubility of the union between Spain and her Colonies," but he added these most eloquent words: "To-day is the last day of old Spain, crushing in her fall the fetters of the slave, and the birthday of that other Spain that by means of her ideas unites herself indissolubly with the America of freedom, of democracy and of right."

His speech was a poem, an ode to progress and liberty.

"If Spain, gentlemen," Castelar cried, "if Spain is to be made up of arbitrary generals, greedy bureaucrats, selfish tax-gatherers, censors who stifle human thought, unbridled hosts massacring children, the slave-trafficker's bark, the Babylon of the plantation, and to crown all this the bazaar and the slave-market—ah! then, arise with me and cry: Accursed be the genius of our country!"

Is it possible that the man whose voice manifested such noble sentiments, to which the harmonious Castillian language gave added enchantment, should now be cursing the genius of a country which will soon accomplish all the reforms which he was begging the Spanish people to bestow? Can this be the same Castelar who twenty-five years after wrote that the Spanish government "could not learn from outsiders its faults in governing the Antilles, or submit to a mediator"? Alas! the principle of the indissolubility of the union between Spain and her Colonies had stifled in him the higher principles which he had expressed in 1873. The new Spain was never born, or else it was a still-birth, and the Republic which was established

SPANISH RULE IN CUBA.

after the abdication of Amadeus did not accomplish the good which had been expected of it. Spain instead of uniting herself to the America of freedom, of democracy and of right, persisted in her attachment to the Cuba of tyranny, of despotism and of wrong.

Here is a sample of the comfort which the Cubans derived from the establishment of the Republic in Spain: "The Spanish government sends salutations to Cuba and Porto Rico, and assures them that the integrity of Spanish territory is to be maintained."

This message proved undoubtedly highly pleasing to the Peninsulars and the Volunteers, but with what enthusiasm the Insular Cubans received the greetings and the magnanimous assurance which they contained, history does not say.

The genius of Spain, of which Castelar spoke in 1873, has had the good luck of being led by the genius of a Genoese sailor to the discovery of a new world; it has slaughtered the people that it found there, then instead of being satisfied with the indirect profits which might reasonably have accrued from a proper administration of Colonial possessions, it has killed the hen that laid the golden eggs.

The genius of Spain is still the genius of Philip II. and of the Duke of Alva; which gave to the world Torquemada and the Inquisition, which laid bare the Low Countries, and tortured and murdered their noble citizens.

The genius of Spain has exercised a most demoralizing influence over that portion of Italy to which it has chiefly extended its operations.[1]

The genius of Spain has practically annihilated one of the most beautiful spots in the world; the Cubans were begging for bread, it has answered their supplications by giving them a stone; it has garroted or otherwise murdered with the semblance of a legal process, during the space of five years only, four thousand six hundred and seventy-two of the inhabitants of Cuba, the offspring of Spanish blood.

And it may be suggested that it is now time for the genius of Spain to take a back seat.

It is reported that ex-Premier Crispi, of Italy, said that the present war is the end of Spain, and if he did, he spoke the truth.

---

[1] See note 7A, page 205.

CHAPTER XII.

The Golden Book of Cuba—The Execution of Leon and Medina—The Treachery of General Mena—A Distinction With a Difference—Two Cuban and One Italian Poets.

For an idea of what the crimes of Spain have been during the period of the ten years' war we must take up the examination of a book to which reference is made by Mr. Halstead in his "Story of Cuba." It is called the "Book of Blood" and was published in 1873, after the war which began in 1868 had run only one-half of its course. It is a record, not indeed of all the Cuban patriots who have been murdered by Spain, which it were impossible to establish, but merely of those who have been "executed," during those five years, after the humbug of a trial and with a pretense of legality. "We do not claim," says the preface, "we do not claim to give a table of the crimes committed in Havana and elsewhere, such for example as those at the theatre of Villanueva, the coffee-house of the

Louvre * * * the butchery of Cohner Greenwald and many like cases; or the transcendentally treacherous killing of Augusto Arango under a flag of truce. Neither shall we attempt to catalogue the murders committed by the brutal soldiery in the country, the indiscriminate slaughter of defenceless men, women and children, the rapes, the obscene mutilations and the cruelties of every kind perpetrated in our unhappy country by the scourge of America; those are personal crimes which we do not deem just to charge upon a whole people."

The "Book of Blood" shows that during the governments of General Lersundi, Dulce, De Rodas, Ceballos, Pieltain and Jovellar, the last three representing the Spanish Republic, four thousand six hundred and seventy-two political prisoners have been killed by the "garrote vil" or by shooting. The names of the victims, as far as it has been possible to ascertain them, are given, also the date of arrest, and the date and place of execution. Here are a few of the entries in that book of Spanish infamy, taken at random.

1870-Dec. 17-Porto Principe—Capt. Francisco Betan- 1,934
    court, Emilio Estrada, Carlos Torres,
    Jose Molina, Francisco Benavides,
    Mannel Montojo y Caballero, Janvier
    B. Varona, Martin Loynazy Miranda, 8-Died Jan. 1, 71
1871-Feb. 20-Juan Sanchez—M. Perdomo and S. Mila,
    A. Paredes, E. Rivero, J. B. Agra-
    monte, J. Martinez, P. Ibarra, B.
    Leiva, and F. Echmeudia, . . .   9-Died Mar. 12.
1871-Feb. 21-La Vega—Jose Manuel Quesada (75 years
    old) for the crime of being uncle to
    General Quesada, ...   1-Died April 1.
1873-Nov. 8-Santiago—Arturo Loret Mola, Augus-
    tin Varona, Oscar Varona, Guil-
    lermo Vals, Jose Boitel, Salvador
    Peuedo, Enrique Castellanos, Augus-
    tin Santa Rosa, Justo Consuegra,
    Francisco Porras Pita, Jose Otero,
    Herminio Quesada, ...   12-Died Nov. 15.

One item gives the names of fifty-five victims, among them Cespedes and Manuel Quesada; another one gives nineteen names.

The "Book of Blood" will become in future years the Golden Book of Cuba; a roll of honor, which the American citizen of the State of Santiago or of Pinar del Rio will anxiously scan for the names of his ancestors who distinguished themselves in the fight for liberty; he may not find them, perhaps, for he will come across items like these:

1870-Dec. 1-Gibara—One who smelt as a rebel, . .   1-Died Dec. 18.
1870-Nov. 27-Siguanea—Alejo Contero, Felix Yuru-
    bide, and thirteen more, ...   15-Died Dec. 18.

1870-Dec. 31-Guanaja—Seven prisoners captured with
 the wife of President Cespedes, . 7-Died Jan. 14.
1871-Feb. 15-Ciego—A rebel, ... 1-Died Mar. 1.
1871-Feb. 19-Sancti Espiritu—A postman, ... 1-Died Mar. 1.
1871-Feb. 23-Guaramena—Seventeen rebels, . . . 17-Died Mar. 17.

Among the victims at Havana in 1869 were two men, one named Leon, the other Medina, who had been sentenced to death for secreting arms. There was an immense crowd to witness the execution, and many among it sympathized with the patriot cause. When Leon reached the scaffold he determined to speak, in spite of an attempt made by the priest to dissuade him. In order to gain a hearing he cried out "Viva España!" (Hurrah for Spain!) which was responded by the huzzas of the Volunteers. He then went on to denounce in a few brief words the tyranny which had condemned him, and finished his speech with enthusiastic "Vivas" for Cuba, independence and Cespedes! The drummers were so astonished that they forgot to drown the remarks with the noise of their drums, as they had been ordered to do in case seditious words were spoken. The soldiers had answered with cheers the first words of the prisoner, but his last ones

Scene at the Execution of Leon and Medina, 1869.

called forth a tumultuous response from the Cubans. In their wrath the Volunteers turned upon the crowd and fired, killing or wounding many people. Mr. Hall, the American Consul, had made efforts to prevent the execution, but had been unsuccessful.

In January, 1869, General Augusto Arango went as a parliamentary under the protection of a flag of truce into the Spanish lines. The Spanish general, Mena, caused him to be shot, then had the body cut to pieces and the fragments paraded through the streets of Puerto Principe.

Heine[1]

> "* * * * a German poet
> Of goodly German fame,"

as he took pride in being, once in a fit of misanthropy laid down the following maxim: "Yes, we ought to forgive our enemies—but not until they are hanged."

The American soldiers and statesmen have done better, and have acted more in accordance with the true and original principles of Christianity; they

---
(1) See note 7, page 204.

SPANISH RULE IN CUBA.

have pardoned without hanging. The Spanish have done worse; they have hanged without pardoning, for they have butchered the bodies of their enemies after life was extinct. Heine said that he would, before their death, forgive his enemies the injuries they had done him during their lives, but Spain did not forgive her enemies even after death, and this did not happen in the fifteenth or sixteenth century, but in our present enlightened age, within the sight of some of us who are not very old yet. The trouble with her is that she has not yet understood that the people whom she has misgoverned may wish to renounce her authority without being necessarily worse than Judas Iscariot. In her eyes, one of her colonists who refuses to acknowledge her dominion is guilty of a crime deserving the most painful death which the body can suffer, in this world, and the eternal burning of the soul in hell, in the next.

Among the Cuban patriots whose life was destroyed by Spain during the course of the ten years' war was one of the most noted American poets of

Spanish lineage. Marco Antonio Canini—the father of the writer of this study—in his work "Il Libro dell'Amore"—The Book of Love—[1](a collection of love poetry of all nations and all times, translated by him from the originals in nearly one hundred and fifty languages into Italian verse) wrote as follows in the critical and philological essay preceding the third volume of that work, published in Venice in 1888: "Among the other Hispano-American songs I recommend above all, those of the Cuban Zenea, whose life has been extinguished by Spain, who is as unforeseeing and unjust in the administration of her Colonies as she is cruel in repressing the attempts at independence. Placido Valdes was another Cuban poet murdered by Spain and I will give some of his verses elsewhere; the first one of those unhappy men addressed his last verses to his wife, the second to his mother."

---

[1] See note 8, page 205.

The King and Queen Regent of Spain.
See note 11, page 207.

CHAPTER XIII.

Public Opinion Abroad—The Forests of Royal Palms Between New York and Washington—The Congressional Express—A Bouquet of Flowers From the Paris Figaro—Ignorance and Vitriol—How a Great Nation is Being Deceived.

Those words of the old Italian patriot and poet have been reported here not only on account of the interesting information which they contain in connection with the scope of this study, but also for the purpose of pointing out that public opinion in most European countries is not, as many suppose, against us in our present conflict; England and Italy,[1] for instance, would not seem to be easily able to find in their history any reason for being particularly friendly to Spain, and there can be only one opinion among liberal-minded and well-informed people the world over as to the justice of our cause, only one hope as to the result, and that for its inevitable success. The holders of Spanish bonds and their advocates are, of course, excluded from the limits of this assertion.

---

[1] See note 12, page 208.

SPANISH RULE IN CUBA.

But the trouble is that a large number of people in Europe entertain some extraordinary ideas in regard to our customs, our habits and things in general in this country, and through lack of proper information about the condition of affairs in the United States, and especially in respect to the Cuban question, are induced to direct their sympathies into the wrong channel.

A short while ago there appeared in the Paris "Figaro," a prominent but hardly respected newspaper, noted for its famous *canards,* what purported to be "The Impressions of a Parisian in the United States." This particular bird began its flight on the 30th of March, continued it on the 1st of April, and concluded it on the 5th of that month. Whether it was intended by the "Figaro" as a present to its readers with the compliments of the season, I do not know, but in that case the peregrination through three issues of the paper was a little too long. The writer spent two weeks in the United States; he went from New York to Washington for the purpose of interviewing President

McKinley, and we will allow him to speak for himself.

"I leave New York on an icy cold morning, and little by little the temperature becomes milder, the thermometer rises—it is spring, soon it is summer. At first forests of pines, then forests of palm trees. —In Washington the thermometer showed 96 in the shade.—Wonderful landscapes where practical life never loses its rights. Here and there suspended from the palm trees, along the road, large signboards with advertisements of the best soap or of the best shoe-blacking."

On arriving in Washington he feels disappointed: "At the depot in Washington, instead of the graceful American girls whom I expected to see, my sight meets only fat and horrible negresses, attired in bloomers, lazily leaning on their wheel."

This is the impression which he will take back to Paris of the Capital of the United States:

"A queer city * * * the impression that we are in the tropics becomes stronger at the sight of so many negroes; they form here the majority of the population."

SPANISH RULE IN CUBA.

But he hurries to the White House:

"I go in as in a public square, and I see neither guardians nor servants—not even a janitor. In the vestibule a sign-board with this mention, and the drawing of a hand pointing in the proper direction, 'Entrance to the Parlor.'"

When he reaches the President he has a very pleasant conversation with him. The President is at first a little restive about talking on the Cuban question, but finally he becomes more communicative. He may, for all we know, have been on the point of asking that bright young man for his opinion and advice, but the reporter is compelled to leave in haste, which is extremely unfortunate for us, as he might have been of great assistance to the President in guiding him through the difficulties which were soon to follow. His hurry was caused by the fact that he had been successful in obtaining a "special permit" which allowed him to take the "Congressional Express," and he did not want to miss it. The Congressional Express, we are informed, is a train which takes back to New York the members of Congress after the day is over, for very few of them live in Washington.

That enterprising representative of a still more enterprising newspaper had probably picked up somewhere on the boulevards an advertisement of the Pennsylvania Railroad, but he did not know that the only permit required in order to travel on the Congressional Express is the possession of one of those little slips of green paper which are so carefully marked with a V or an X at the Department of the Treasury in that same city of Washington which he claims to have visited; and while those permits are entirely too scarce to suit most of us they are not particularly "special."

When he got back to New York "bands of excited individuals" were running through the streets yelling, "Death to the Spaniards!" "It was enough for any one to state that he was a Cuban citizen in order to be walked about from saloon to saloon, and compelled to swallow cocktails without number." By such indications New York will soon be empty of New Yorkers, only Cubans will be found in that city.

SPANISH RULE IN CUBA.

The whole thing was evidently intended for a hoax, and it was a display of cheap wit. The reporters of the "Figaro" did not always find the vestibule to the White House entirely deserted, for that paper stated—and this time quite seriously—that the Officer who took to the President the report of the Board of Inquiry on the Maine had, on entering the White House, to make his way, "revolver in hand, through a crowd of idlers." [1]

It was the "Figaro," if I am not mistaken, which years ago, when the Republican party was divided into two camps, the Stalwarts and the Half Breeds, explained to its readers that the latter were "the great cattle-raisers of the West," having most likely been misled by a literal application of the word "breeding."

But the blunders of the "Figaro" and other European newspapers are not always so innocent. Here are some samples of the literature on which intelligent people in Europe are expected to base their opinion with regard to the attitude of the United

---
(1) Le Figaro, March 27, 1898.

States on the Cuban question; the four that follow are taken from different issues of the same paper.

"The Spaniards are wise, they have proved it, and nothing shows that they will play into the hands of unscrupulous men who speculate on their chivalrous sentiments."

"One may conceive a war aiming at the triumph of intangible principles, or of commercial interests of the greatest importance, but it cannot be conceived in order to facilitate speculations on the sale of tobacco, of sugar or of poor American newspapers."

"The American jingoes—Senators engaged in speculations in sugar and in tobacco, Representatives who wish to flatter the unconscious mob, members of Cuban insurrectional committees composed of buyers at a trifling price of lands devastated by the civil war, continue in Washington and New York their campaign of excitation and of slander."

"It is the entire archipelago of the West Indies that they are hungry for."[1]

Another prominent Parisian newspaper, "La

---
[1] See note 8, page 206.

SPANISH RULE IN CUBA. 151

Paix"—"The Peace"—under date of April 30th, has an article which begins by praising Cuba for "struggling desperately against the tyrannical domination of bigoted and retrograde Spain." "Europe," says the editor, "should have intervened long ago in behalf of Cuba agonizing under the bloody rule of Spain. But it seems that under the same pretext of respect for international law, or I know not what stupid protocol, the powers have been content to witness that barbarous struggle between Spain and Cuba." Here, however, the talented editor turns the search-light of his investigation on this benighted country: "As to one point there can be no doubt," continues the writer in "La Paix," "the intervention of the United States in Cuban affairs is justified by no international code."

In other words, Europe (3,000 miles away or over) should have intervened in Cuba and would have been justified by international law, for it was only under a pretext of respect for it that she has not done it. In the case of the United States (100 miles from the Cuban coast or thereabouts), however, intervention is decidedly contrary to that same law. Europe is to be blamed for not interfering on account of some stupid protocol, but that same stupid protocol should inspire us with veneration and with awe. The why and wherefore of all this constitute a problem which my mind cannot solve, and the reader may, if he likes, figure it out for himself; but from a superficial examination it would seem that "The Peace" is at war—with common sense.

Our friend, the editor of "La Paix," then continues to pay his respects to the United States, and delivers himself of the following tirade, which the Chicago "Inter-Ocean" of May 8th, where it is reported, properly characterizes as ignorant and vitriolic: "If civilized Europe had been mindful of her duty and her dignity, if she had been moved by conscience and self-interest, she would long ago have forced the United States to take her ships from Cuban ports and would have imposed peace on the combatants. As for the United States no scruples of conscience embarrass that nation of brigands. The Yankees care nothing for the interest and dignity of civilization. It amuses them to talk of Christian civilization, but the prime motive behind their declaration of war is the desire to acquire Cuba and become the foremost producers of sugar. The least discerning have been struck by the mixture of hypocrisy and brutality which characterizes the diplomatic and military action of the United States."

The least discerning would be struck by the fact that to characterize the noble and dignified efforts of President McKinley to maintain the peace as hypocrisy, and the firm action which necessarily followed their failure, as brutality, is to make a remarkable display of asininity. The editor of "La Paix" is mistaken; it does not amuse the Yankees to talk of Christian civilization; what amuses them to the point of extravagant hilarity is to listen to the aberrant and discrepant jabber of a man who knows as much about their affairs and their history as Christopher Columbus knew about those of the Great Khan of the Indies, whose acquaintance he expected to make when he first landed in Cuba.

That is, it would amuse them, were it not for the fact that it is on such rot that the opinion of an intelligent, a great and generous people like the French nation, is being formed, and that that nation is thus induced to attribute to us motives and purposes which are as far removed from our minds as the shores of France are geographically distant from those of Columbia.

Ex'mo Sr. Don Praxedes Mateo Sagasta,
President of the Spanish Cabinet.

CHAPTER XIV.

The Situation in Cuba After the Peace of El Zanjon—Outbreak of the Present Revolution—Jose Marti, His Work, His Death and His Burial—How Matters Stood in Cuba in April, 1898—The Brilliant Ideas of General Weyler—Why Autonomy is Not Acceptable.

The reforms which had been granted by the Treaty of El Zanjon had, as we have seen, proved entirely delusive. The same state of affairs prevailed in Cuba after Gomez and the other leaders of the ten years' war had been induced to capitulate, as had existed for four hundred years previously, with the single exception of the condition of slavery. The despotic policy called the policy of the "Realidad nacional" was continued; the representation of Cuba in the Cortes was useless, because the votes of the Cuban deputies were not allowed to count in matters of importance, besides the Peninsulars were able to control the polls, and all but a few of the deputies were natives of Spain; the governors still enjoyed the same absolute power. Industry was discouraged, for it would have interfered with the interests of the Spanish manufacturing cities. The taxes were as heavy, or heavier, than ever and they were still applied to the benefit of the mother country. No intention was shown of giving the Cubans the part that properly belonged to them in the administration of their island; that administration continued to be as corrupt as it had ever been and the secret exactions of its officials were still based on the idea of making as much money as possible before returning to Spain. As an example of its operations I will quote the following lines from the Introduction by Mr. John Fiske to Mr. Grover Flint's book "Marching with Gomez:"

"A planter's estate is entered upon the assessor's lists as worth $50,000; the collector comes along and demands a tax based upon an assumed value of $70,000; the planter demurs, but presently thinks it prudent to compromise upon a basis of $60,000. No change is made in the published lists, but the collector slips into his own pocket the tax upon $10,000 and goes away rejoicing. Thus the planter is robbed while the government is cheated. And this is a fair specimen of what goes on throughout all departments of administration. From end to end the whole system is honeycombed with fraud."

It is related by Mathurin M. Ballou in his book "Due South," published in 1885, that within recent years an issue of Cuban currency having been authorized by the Madrid government to be printed in an establishment in the United States, the Cuban officials had notes to the extent of fourteen million dollars printed over and above the authorized amount, and shared that sum among themselves. It is not surprising to hear that the Captain-General, a worthy successor of the residenciado governors of the sixteenth century and of General Tacon, who was a poor man when he landed in Cuba, returned to Spain several times a millionaire.

Such conditions, and those produced by the unfair laws regulating foreign commerce, could not fail to result in the utter ruination of the economical interests of the Island. In fact, the insurrection which was shortly to follow may be said to be due principally to a necessity for economic relief, rather than to the desire for political liberty which accompanied it. In 1890, addresses were sent to the home government by the majority of the agricultural and other associations of the island, stating their grievances and asking for certain remedies; later a delegation was sent to Madrid, but all the efforts made by the Insular Cubans to obtain an amelioration of their condition came to nothing; Spain continued to turn a deaf ear to their protests; in fact the evils were rather aggravated than otherwise.

Thus, the Insulars were brought to rebel another time against their iniquitous mother country, and took up again the arms which they had been induced to lay down in 1878 by her lying promises.

The cry of "Cuba libre!" (free Cuba) was raised by a band of about thirty men under the leadership of Antonio Lopez Coloma, in the neighborhood of Ibarra, province of Matanzas, on the 24th of February, 1895, and on the same day an uprising took place in Baires and in Jiguany, near Santiago. The revolution into which these two outbreaks developed was due principally to the influence of Josi Marti, who has been called its father. He was a born conspirator, and since childhood had been devoted to the cause of the independence of his country; he had organized "Juntas" among the Cubans in almost every city in the United States in order to help the insurrection which he had for years been meditating. Several patriots of the ten years' war landed at Baracoa on March 31st, among them Antonio and Jose Maceo. On April 11th, Maximo Gomez and Marti himself landed on the same spot. Marti was killed in battle on the 19th of May. His body was taken to Santiago by the Spaniards, and the words which were spoken over his remains at the burial by the Spanish Colonel Sandoval manifest sentiments so exceptionally different from those which have almost invariably inspired the actions of Spain, that they cause the student of the history of Cuba to feel as refreshed as a man who meets with an oasis in traveling through a desert, and they deserve to be reported here to the honor of that officer.[1]

"Gentlemen:—In presence of the corpse of him who in life was Jose Marti, and in the absence of any relative or friend who might speak over his remains such words as are customary, I request you not to consider these remains to be those of an enemy any more, but simply those of a man carried by political discords to face Spanish soldiers. From the moment the spirits have freed themselves of matter, they are sheltered and magnanimously pardoned by the Almighty, and the abandoned matter is left in our care, for us to dispel all rancorous feelings, and give the corpse such Christian burial as is due to the dead."

Gomez invaded the province of Puerto Principe, his old battle ground; subsequently he directed the movements in the East, and Maceo those in the West. Calixto Garcia, another veteran of the ten years' war was and is still another prominent leader. His forehead bears to this day the scar of the wound which he inflicted upon himself when, dur-

---

[1] The speech is taken from Halstead's Story of Cuba, page 266.

Cuban General
Rius Rivera.

Cuban General
Quintin Bandera.

Cuban Cabecilla (Chief)
Jesus Rabi.

Cuban Sentry.

ing the course of that war, he attempted to take his own life, because, like the Siboneyes of old, he preferred to die rather than to fall into the hands of the Spaniards; however, he did not succeed, and although his life was spared by the enemies, he was made acquainted with the horrors of a Spanish prison. Antonio Maceo was killed in 1896. He was a colored man, and had been the last one of the leaders of the previous revolution to lay down his arms; it is said that his father, who afterwards was killed during the war of 1868-1878, after his farm had been burned by the Spaniards, at that time had made his children swear on its ruins that they would consecrate their lives to the liberation of their country. After Maceo's death Maximo Gomez assumed supreme command of the revolutionary army.

It would be necessary to go beyond the limits set to this study in order to follow in detail all the events of this revolution, and to pick out of the confusing multitude of contradictory news which was received of this war such of it as was wheat and such as was chaff; it will be enough for our purpose to say that Senator Proctor who made lately a personal investigation of the condition of affairs in the Island ascertained that out of the 200,000 soldiers which Spain sent to Cuba since the beginning of the rebellion in 1895, only 60,000 remained fit for duty at the time of his visit. On the other hand it is stated, on good authority, that out of the 1,500,000 inhabitants which the Island contained in 1895 only 900,000 are left alive. The prisoners made by the Spaniards are invariably shot; the revolutionists at first spared the lives of the prisoners who fell into their hands, but later have done the same as their enemies; disease and starvation do the rest. The rebels burn the canefields so that no export duty may be collected on the sugar produced by the Island to increase the resources of the enemy, and so that no money from its sale may come into Cuba and find its way to Spain in payment for purchases of Spanish manufactures; they destroy farms and wreck villages.

The Spaniards ruin and burn everything that is left in order to deprive the insurgents of the means

SPANISH RULE IN CUBA.

of obtaining a subsistence. Spain has conclusively shown that she is unable to put an end to the insurrection, and had the United States allowed the situation to be prolonged indefinitely the story of the Kilkenny cats, which was recalled in this connection by a correspondent of the "London Times," would have been particularly appropriate in describing the situation, since neither a Spaniard nor a Cuban would have been left to tell the tale, and the Island would have consisted of a mound of skeletons on a mass of ruins.

Soon after the revolution broke out, Spain sent Marshal Martinez Campos to subdue it, but the Cubans had grown suspicious of Spaniards who came to them with an offer of presents, and besides, here again as formerly in the case of General Dulce, the Peninsulars and the Volunteers were dissatisfied with the Marshal's comparative lack of severity, and they still controlled the situation. After a short time, Campos was recalled and General Weyler was sent to take his place, with a commission which gave him absolute authority over the Island.

166 FOUR CENTURIES OF

Hernando De Soto.
From an engraving in Herrera's
Historia General, (edition of 1728).

General Valeriano Weyler.

General Martinez Campos.

Spanish General Pando.

SPANISH RULE IN CUBA.

The atrocities perpetrated by Don Valeriano Weyler, a Spaniard of Austrian descent, who will go down to posterity under the surname of "the butcher,"[1] are in everyone's memory. This Austro-Spaniard, in whom seem to have descended the cruel instincts both of a Radetzky and of a Duke of Alva, had an idea which, had he been born in another age, might have been considered a stroke of genius; it was the idea of tearing thousands upon thousands of peaceful men, women and children from their homes in the fields, of dragging them into the cities, and of leaving them there to starve, so that they might not give any comfort to the cause of the enemy he was fighting. Unfortunately for Weyler, he was born too late, such talent is not appreciated in our times, save perhaps, in his own country; in every other part of the civilized world it is regarded with feelings of abhorrence.

The man who could not conquer Cuba with one hundred thousand soldiers or more, now boasts that he can conquer the United States with fifty thou-

---

[1] Weyler inherited this title from the General Count of Balmaseda, to whom it was given during the ten years' war--See also note 9, page 206.

sand, and the surprise with which we are listening to his utterances is somewhat similar to that which was once experienced by Balaam.

Weyler arrived in Havana February 10, 1896; he at once issued a proclamation announcing that the utmost severity would be the ruling spirit of his administration; by his orders military tribunals took the place of civil courts, and a few days after his arrival, he inaugurated his reign by causing a number of political prisoners in Cabanas to be shot. It was then that Gomez and Maceo proclaimed that if Weyler would kill prisoners they would retaliate by killing every Spanish soldier who might fall into their hands.

Another idea in which Weyler placed great confidence besides that of reconcentrating into the cities, Pacificos, or countrymen, who were noncombatants, was that of the famous Trocha. This is a system of military roads extending in several directions in the Island and supposed to form a barrier which the insurgents would be entirely unable to pass. Gomez, during the ten years' war passed it seven times and, on one occasion, even took his wife and his children along. Balmaseda had a poor opinion of the Trocha, and said that he would not have it even for a gift, but Campos and especially Weyler, who largely extended it, greatly relied on this obsolete strategic device, which has been justly compared to a China wall in point of utility. The Trocha was crossed several times by the Cuban leaders. In spite of it Gomez invaded Matanzas and Havana provinces; Maceo marched into Pinar del Rio; then for a time both generals disappeared, and Weyler published a bulletin declaring the Provinces of Havana and Pinar del Rio free of insurgents. Immediately Maceo returned, sacked and burned the port of Batabano, to the south of Havana, and began a second invasion of Pinar del Rio; within six weeks he had entered or destroyed nearly every town, city and village in the province.

When a commission was sent to Havana to solicit from General Weyler some government aid for the destitute people who were starving in the cities where he had driven the Reconcentrados, his answer was: "Nothing, the people must bow their heads." In an interview with a lady representing an American newspaper, Mrs. Masterson, he was asked whether the stories that had been published of his cruelty could be denied, and he merely shrugged his shoulders and said that "such things were not important."

Despite the small importance which he gave to the life of his fellow-beings, Weyler could accomplish nothing, and Spain finally decided to recall him and to send a milder man in his place. It was too late. General Blanco became Captain-General and Weyler returned home declaring that the Spanish government had yielded in a cowardly manner to the insolent demands of the United States. Later, a scheme of Autonomy for Cuba was formed by Spain, and it was sought to put it into practice. Had such a reform been granted thirty, or even twenty years ago, and had Spain faithfully observed its provisions, the problem would most likely have been satisfactorily solved. But the time for such a thing had passed; the Cubans had come to distrust Spain more than ever in consequence of her actions after the peace of El Zanjon, and their leaders, among whom there are of course some excellent scholars, remembered the old saying, "Timeo Danaos et dona ferentes,"[1] and applied its philosophy to the scheme of Autonomy as they had applied it to the blandishments of Martinez Campos on his second visit to the Island; and so the destruction, the ruin and the death still went merrily on on both sides.

[1] This verse from Virgil's Æneid has been translated as follows: "The Greeks I fear, and most when gifts they bring."

172   FOUR CENTURIES OF

General Blanco,
Probably the last of the Spanish
Captain-Generals in Cuba.

Admiral Segismundo Bermejo,
Spanish Ex-Minister of Marine.

Don Segismundo Moret y
Prendergast,
Spanish Ex-Minister of the Colonies.

Don Alberto Aguilera y
Velasco,
Civil Governor of Madrid.

CHAPTER XV.

The Feeling at Home—Autonomy—The Situation in the Winter of 1897-98.

The representatives of the American people manifested several times since the present revolution broke out the universal feeling in the United States in regard to the Cuban question by introducing and discussing in Congress many resolutions proclaiming the sentiment of this nation that Cuba had the right to shake off the infamous and detested Spanish yoke. Thus, during the first session of the Fifty-fourth Congress concurrent resolutions were passed suggesting to the President the advisability of recognizing the insurgents as belligerent forces and also advising him to negotiate with Spain towards securing the independence of the Island. The Foreign Relations Committee of the Senate adopted resolutions acknowledging independence, and they were reported by Senator Cameron on the 21st of December, 1896. Later, the Senate passed by a vote of 41 to 14 a joint resolution, declaring that war existed in Cuba, and that the government should accord the rights of belligerents to the insurgents, but the two branches of Congress did not come together as to the terms in which such a resolution should be passed. Both Mr. Cleveland and Mr. McKinley, however, followed in this regard the precedent left by the Administration of President Grant during the ten years' war, and constantly refused to acknowledge either the belligerency of the insurgents or the independence of the State which the latter claimed to have organized, for the same reasons that directed the policy of the United States during that war. The revolutionists had, it is true, an appearance of civil government, with a House of Representatives and an Administration, Salvador Cisneros being President and Bartolomé Maso, Vice-President, the latter afterwards succeeding Cisneros in the Presidency, and the capital was said to be at Cubitas, but it was evident that the so-called government had no power to enforce its decisions, and was rather the expression of a desire

SPANISH RULE IN CUBA. 175

for such a government than a government in reality.

With the loyalty which has always characterized the action of the United States in the Cuban question the President issued, in June, 1896, a proclamation of neutrality, warning the citizens of this country that they should not aid the insurgents; and, for this, General Weyler soon after returned thanks by assuming to abrogate the contracts of Cubans with Americans and by claiming the right to imprison American citizens, and even put them to death.

Notwithstanding the President's proclamation, the Administration found it extremely difficult, as it had on previous occasions to prevent the organization of filibustering expeditions, and although it exerted its powers to their full extent in that direction many such expeditions were, nevertheless, organized in this country; for as Mr. Bayard had written in 1885 to Minister Valera, "this government does not and cannot undertake, as I have shown, to control the workings of opinion; sympathy and affiliation of sentiments and the expression thereof are not punishable in this country by law," and it was that affiliation of sentiments which found an expression in the getting up of expeditions in aid of the revolutionists, and in dealing leniently with the violators of the law whenever they were caught. Many complications followed on this account, and in this connection may be mentioned the case of the bark "Competitor," which came near being a repetition of the "Virginius" affair.

At last Spain formulated a plan of Autonomy for the Island, and sought to put it in operation; but it was unacceptable to the Insular Cubans for the reasons which have been told in the preceding chapter; the insurgents considered the offer as a mere device of Spain to induce them to lay down their arms. Nevertheless President McKinley endeavored to persuade the Cubans to give the plan a trial, and he insisted in his message of December, 1897, that the new liberal government of Spain should have an opportunity of trying the effect, in the island, of a new and more humane policy, which Captain-General Blanco was supposed to represent;

SPANISH RULE IN CUBA. 177

The Latest Portrait of Maximo Gomez.
Maximo Gomez.
Colonel Bosco.
(From La Illustracion Espanola.)

but the President emphatically asserted the right of this country to intervene in case the insurrection should be prolonged, notwithstanding the reforms promised by the Spaniards.

And while the President of the United States was making these most generous efforts to maintain the peace, and restrain the impatience of his people, giving in these circumstances a proof of such statesmanship as must entitle him to the respect and approval of even his political enemies, the orgy of Death was going on in the fair Island at our doors.

The Cuban mothers were raising their hands in prayer to God, and fervently hoping in the United States for the execution of His will.[1] Spain was talking of her honor and of her dignity. Part of Europe was looking on, unconscious; another part was softly murmuring its sympathy, but was keeping its hands in its pockets; another still, was praising the chivalry of Spain, remembering her old traditions, asserting her rights. Here and there, in the dark, Spanish bonds were lurking.

---

[1] "Men and women existed in dull unceasing dread, praying that Mr. Cleveland, *who could do anything*, would interfere to help them." —Grover Flint—"Marching with Gomez," page 100.

SPANISH RULE IN CUBA.

In this country, the case was different. Here the people—the mass of the American people—cared nothing for the more or less disinterested talk of sensational newspapers, cared still less for the interests of Wall street speculators, for those of the Sugar Trust, or for those of the holders of either Spanish or Cuban bonds. Their one, single, obstinate idea was that a carousal of blood was going on within one hundred miles of their land of liberty; that a brave people preferred their own extermination to giving up the same inalienable rights which have created this nation, and that no hope, no trust was to be placed in Spain for sincerity and truthfulness. The danger to peace was great; a very small spark might have given rise to a great conflagration; but the spark did not come.

There came, instead, a thunderbolt.

CHAPTER XVI.

The Maine—The Outcome of a Commercial Inclination —Why Arbitration was not Resorted To—A Different Interpretation of Words—How Revolutions Should be Opposed—Freedom at Last—Why We Are At War With Spain—The Genius of America—The Future Destinies of Cuba.

The destruction of the ship which, as the "Illustracion Española" rather ironically said, "was sent to us in an evil hour by the courtesy of the North American people," broke the last vestige of patience which Uncle Sam had left.

In the same spirit of fairness and impartiality which causes us to say that we must give his dues even to the Prince of Darkness we are not prepared to assert at the present time that the terrible event of the 15th of February, 1898—happened with the connivance of the Spanish officials, for before such an assertion is made undoubted proofs thereof should be secured, which, so far, has not been done; perhaps it never will, so that the real cause of the explosion of the "Maine" is likely to remain a mystery forever.

The Destruction of the "Maine," Feb. 15, 1898.

But whether it happened through the guilt of Spain, or was the action of one or more fanatics acting independently and without the knowledge of the Spanish authorities, the fact remains that Spain has been negligent or powerless in not preventing the outrage. If she has been negligent she deserves punishment, if powerless, then authority in Cuba should be placed in more competent hands. Spain has been clamorously protesting and expressing her indignation at the suspicions which were directed against her, and these protests, which have, it must be said, all the appearance of being sincere, are entitled to consideration; but at the same time it must be remembered that history shows us that Spain is naturally cruel and given to not observing her compacts, and for that reason those of us who listen to her shrieks with a little incredulity may properly be excused for so doing. As to the supposition that the explosion may have been altogether accidental, it is entirely excluded by the report of our Board of Inquiry, which was composed of competent men who investigated the subject thoroughly.

SPANISH RULE IN CUBA.

However it may be, it is certain that the exasperation provoked in the American people by that horrible loss and the cruel death of about two hundred and sixty-six brave men precipitated matters and determined an intervention justified in every way by the circumstances; at any rate, the "New York Herald" has lately made this interesting calculation, which the Spaniards will not fail to attribute to the commercial spirit of this nation:

Total cost of Spanish men-of-war destroyed at Manila, May 1, 1898... $8,400,000

Total cost of the Maine............ 4,689,000

Balance in our favor, $3,711,000

And it is most likely that when the final settlement is made, at the end of the war, the ledger will show a still handsomer balance to our advantage.

It has been said that we should have allowed the question of the "Maine" to be settled by arbitration. Perhaps. Mr. Fish in a cablegram to Minister Sickles at the time of the "Virginius" affair stated that when the subject is one of national honor the question is not one for arbitration; the same view lately prevented the ratification by the U. S. Senate of an Arbitration Treaty between this country and Great Britain. It is a mistaken view; arbitration is the proper way to settle any question, no matter of what importance or whatever may be the subject involved; indeed, the graver the question, the greater the call for arbitration, and this will, let us hope, come to be acknowledged at no very distant time by all civilized nations. We do not, in this country, consider duels as a means of settling quarrels involving a matter of honor among individuals; we think, in fact, that we have gone a step further in civilization than most other nations because we do not so recognize it. Why, then, should we claim that it is the only way of settling such questions among people? But we have behind us the history of four centuries which says that the course which it would have been proper to follow had our quarrel been with England, France, Germany or any other nation, was extremely difficult, not to say impossible, in the case of Spain.

SPANISH RULE IN CUBA. 185

Spain promised the Indians that she would stop slaughtering them, but she continued to butcher them, and while she was doing so, she was talking of her honor and dignity.[1]

Spain delayed answering and evaded our just and reasonable claims in the case of the "Black Warrior," and a hundred others of the same kind during that period, till she obtained her object of not giving the United States the satisfaction she owed them.

Spain promised and assured us that General Dulce's order would be revoked, and that the participants in filibustering expeditions would not be treated as pirates; and still fifty-three of the crew of the "Virginius" were wickedly murdered, and one hundred more would have been killed had it not been for the timely interference of English and American cannons.

Spain undertook the obligation of giving us a reparation by saluting our flag, and of otherwise giving us some satisfaction for the "Virginius" out-

---
[1] See note 10, page 207.

rage, but she succeeded in beating us out of everything except the payment of a paltry sum of money, and she laughed in her sleeve while she still talked of her honor and dignity.

Spain promised the Cubans, in 1878, ample reforms and thus obtained that they should give up their fight against her. She gave them the reforms, but they had a string attached to them. Spain, while she stood on her honor and dignity, pulled that string, and, presto! the reforms disappeared.

What guarantee would we have had, that Spain, had we submitted the question of the "Maine" to a Tribunal of Arbitration, would have faithfully abided by the decision of that Tribunal and not tried to evade it in some way? What assurance could Spain give us that she was more sincere in offering a scheme of Autonomy to Cuba than she had been twenty years ago at El Zanjon?

Honor and Dignity! Spain has had for centuries her mouth full of those words, and she has been acting all along with regard to Cuba and the United

SPANISH RULE IN CUBA.

States, savagely and unfaithfully; there is such a vast distance between the value which is placed on them by the American people and the manner in which they have been understood by the various governments of Spain that it were a hopeless task to endeavor to fill it.

And here, I wish to introduce to the reader a good, old Italian proverb: "Le cose che vanno per le lunghe diventano serpi"—"Things that are delayed and long drawn out end by becoming snakes." No good can come of them. Whenever questions have arisen between Spain and the United States she has delayed, and postponed, and evaded, until the results, as far as the United States are concerned, have invariably been—"snakes."

But we could not allow the question of the "Maine" to assume that aspect; no other nation would have done it, and none could reasonably have expected the United States to do it; neither could we allow the devastation and wholesale murder in Cuba to go on indefinitely, and these are the reasons for which we are at present at war with

Spain, since she refused to acknowledge her errors and to see what all the rest of the entire world has clearly perceived, that in the nineteenth century there is no place in this hemisphere for the remnant of a system which would have disgraced the middle ages.

Sixty or seventy years ago, an Italian statesman, Cesare Alfieri, said that "revolutions must be opposed by reform—ample reform."[1] The wisdom of that principle has not been recognized by Spain; she has persistently refused to grant any reform until after having been dragged to do it by force, thinking that it was below her dignity to grant it of her own free will; then her promises, grudgingly given, have been unfaithfully kept, and besides, even supposing that her intentions were sincere, the new colonial scheme came too late to be of any avail. It is to this mistaken sense of honor and dignity, to this blind obstinacy, that Spain largely owes her present plight.

On the 18th of April, 1898, the memorable day on

---

[1] From late indications it would seem that this principle might be profitably applied in the country where it originated.

which the Congress of the United States proclaimed "that the Cuban people are, and of right ought to be, free and independent," the death-knell of Spanish domination in America was tolled. Will Cuba attain true liberty and establish sound and lasting republican institutions, such as we possess, and which may give her freedom, happiness and prosperity if she decides to form a separate nation, with a separate government of her own after the last Spanish soldier has been driven from the Island?

Our own American nation is a composite body, formed chiefly by the very best elements of old Europe. On the positive, practical and daring spirit of the Anglo-Saxon have been grafted the perseverance of the Teuton and of the Scandinavian, the fier inclination of the Celt, and, more recently, idealistic and artistic tendencies of the Italian; from the blending of these various elements, which balance and complete each other, a type has been formed, and is still in course of formation, which will continue to improve with time, after some asperities have been rounded, and after it becomes still more homogeneous.

Not so with the Cubans; they are of one and the same European blood, it is that of their oppressors, and the large infusion of the blood of an ignorant and inferior race like the negro has certainly not done anything toward improvement. By the natural law of heredity, the Cuban inherits the good qualities of the Spaniard—courage and patriotism—but he must also reflect his imperfections; if the truth is to be told, it must be acknowledged that cruelty has not existed only on the Spanish side during the horrible contest.

License and anarchy, not true liberty, is the state of things which prevails in most of the smaller countries of Central and South America, which can hardly be called Republics, but rather caricatures of a Republic, rent as they continually are by revolutions, torn by factions and arbitrarily ruled by whoever may have the force of obtaining the power, while the will of the majority peacefully expressed and implicitly obeyed, on which are based such free institutions as the ones which we enjoy, is totally disregarded. Such is the condition of affairs which would in all certainty prevail in Cuba, should she conclude to establish a separate government for herself. The large proportion of the negroes in the population of the Island should also be considered. The fear was once expressed that by becoming Africanized, Cuba would be a source of danger to the United States; the causes which gave rise to that fear do not exist any more, still the ends of humanity and the cause of civilization would not be served by the creation of a second Hayti, and we may for the welfare of the Island itself properly feel some apprehension in that respect; left to herself it would probably continue to be an eye-sore to the civilized world in general, and to the United States in particular.

The lone star of Cuba has been gravitating for a long time towards the pleiades on our national emblem; it should find its place on it by the side of what was once the lone star of Texas, and it should reach it by a more direct route.

We cannot be accused of having gone into this

war for want of more territory. The fair Hawaiian Islands have been begging us for years to take them into our family, and we have not made up our mind yet whether we will accept them or not. Slavery died long ago; the conditions which it created have ceased to exist; most of us are not particularly anxious for Cuban sugar; some interests in this country might obtain an advantage through the annexation of the Island, but others would just as surely be injured. In a general way the only advantage which we may find either in the independence or annexation of Cuba is the restoration of our legitimate commerce with it which has been utterly ruined by the long and ferocious conflict; a very important objection has been raised in this country to the annexation on the ground that an undesirable element would be introduced in the population of the United States. This, however, in my opinion, although it may have been true long ago, should not be feared at the present time, because the food which would kill a child may properly be assimilated by the body of a man, and because it has

SPANISH RULE IN CUBA.

been sufficiently demonstrated that white and African blood will not mix to any extent in this country.

Thus, whatever there may be of unworthiness in American politics it did not inspire this war, in spite of the assertions of a few ignorant or prejudiced foreign newspapers. It was inspired by the same genius which prompted the thirteen colonies to declare themselves free from the mother country, the genius which, as Thomas Jefferson had prophesied nearly one hundred years ago, built "such an empire for liberty as she has never surveyed since the creation;" the genius which abolished slavery; it is the same genius which preserved the peace in 1854 which has broken it in 1898, the genius of that America which Castelar in his prime called "the America of freedom, of democracy and of right."

To would-be witticisms, to idiotic slander and base insinuations the American people can answer by pointing with pride to these words which were written in 1853 by the Secretary of State of the United States, Mr. Marcy, to the American Minister at

Bivouac, at a Spanish Outpost.

Paris, Mr. Buchanan; it forms part of the correspondence between the Administration of this country at that time and one of its agents; it is not hypocrisy, for, when written, the lines were not intended for the sight of the public:

"It is true that we have in the last half-century greatly enlarged our territory, and so have Great Britain and France enlarged theirs, but we have done it in a manner that may proudly challenge the most rigid scrutiny of mankind. In our territorial expansion, international law has been observed, the rights of others rigorously respected; nothing in short has been done to justify the slightest suspicion of rapacity. The Government of the United States is not unwilling to submit its whole public conduct in this, or indeed in all other respects, to the most scrupulous examination."

These noble words, true in 1853, are still true in 1898, and the unanimity with which the representatives of this nation have, irrespective of the different interests of the various regions whence they had been sent to Congress, voted for the measure which determined the present hostilities, should alone be sufficient to convince the most obdurate doubter that the motives of the American nation are honorable and honest.

We are not bent on a war of conquest; we disclaim all intention of selfish interest; we do not need and are not seeking any expansion of territory. We will give the Cubans entire freedom in the choice of their future destinies; but if they are wise, after gaining their liberty they will decide to preserve it by joining our Union. And if they are practically unanimous in their desire of doing so, we shall not deny them that privilege.

Then, and then only, will the "Queen of the Antilles" know again the peace and the rest which she has not known since her simple and primitive inhabitants first greeted the strangers who came to her in their search for gold.

NOTES.

1

Seventy-seven different portraits of Columbus were gathered at the Columbian Historical Exposition, which was held in Madrid in 1892-93, and none of them bore any material resemblance to the others. Mr. Wm. E. Curtis, assistant to the Commissioner-General for the United States at that Exposition, who was in charge of the historical section, said in his report that "there is no evidence that the features of Columbus have ever been painted or engraved by anyone during his life," and that "the date of the earliest picture that pretended to represent him was six years later than his death. His portrait has been painted, like that of the Madonna and the Saints, by many famous artists each dependent upon the verbal description given of the man by contemporaneous writers and each conveying to the canvas his own conception of what the great seaman's face must have been; but it may not be said that any of the portraits are genuine and it is believed that all of them are more or less fanciful." * * *

"The only portrait which is positively known to have been drawn during the life of the discoverer was a caricature, the sketch of La Cosa, the pilot, and is known as "The La Cosa Vignette." Juan de la Cosa was the pilot of Columbus, and made the first chart of the West Indies. It was drawn on an oxhide and is inscribed "Juan de la Cosa la fijo en el Puerto de Sta. Maria, en el ano de 1500" (made it in the Port of Santa Maria in the year 1500). At the top, in the center, is a rude vignette drawn with an ordinary pen and an awkward hand, representing St. Christopher bearing the Christ child across a stream, and meant to be symbolic of Columbus carrying Christianity to the new world. It was one of the legends of the day that La Cosa intended to give St. Christopher the features of Columbus. Baron von Humboldt, who had heard of the chart, found it in Paris in 1832, in the library of Herr Valcknaer, from whom it was purchased by the Spanish government, and it now hangs in the Naval Museum at Madrid."

(*Executive Documents of the House of Representatives for the Third Session of the Fifth-third Congress, 1894-95, Vol. 31st.*)

"The upholders of the movement to procure the canonization of Columbus, like De Lorgues, have claimed that La Cosa represented the features of Columbus in the face of St. Christopher." (Justin Winsor, History of America, Vol. 2d, page 71.)

2

Individually, in private life and in social intercourse, the Spaniards are charming people, or at least many or most of them are, and no prejudice should be entertained against them in that regard, for there are among them many kind, distinguished and highly cultured men. I wish to remember particularly here in this respect Don Jose Blanco and Don Juliano Principe, the former Consul, the latter Vice Consul for Spain at Philadelphia, in 1878; both are long since dead, and were among the most accomplished gentlemen whom it has ever been my fortune to meet. But the spirit of the Nation is cruel and way behind the times.

3

Bartholomew de Las Casas was born at Seville in 1474 and went to the Indies with Columbus in 1498, returning to Cadiz in 1500. He re-embarked with him in 1502, and was ordained Priest by the Bishop of Hispaniola in 1510, being the first ecclesiastic ordained in the so-called Indies to say there his virgin mass. In his writings he called himself the "Clerigo" (the clergyman) and soon won the title of Universal Protector of the Indians. He returned to Spain in 1515, but went back to the new world in the following year; he also made a number of other trips back and forth, finally returning to Spain in 1547.

His principal work bears, in English, the following title: "A Relation of the first Voyage and Discoveries made by the Spaniards in America—With an account of the Unparalleled Cruelties on the Indians in the Destruction of above Forty Millions of people—together with the Propositions offered to the King of Spain to prevent the further Ruin of the West Indies, By Don Bartholomew de las Casas, Bishop of Chiapa, who was an eye-witness of their cruelties." It was finished at Valencia in 1542, near the beginning of the reign of Philip II. to whom it was dedicated. In the thirty "Propositions" which he laid before the King he claimed that the Kings of Spain held the right of sovereignty in the Indies from the Pope, who "derived from Christ authority and power extending over all men, believers or infidels, in matters pertaining to salvation and eternal life," and who in order to propogate the gospel must avail himself of the help of Christian princes. "The means for establishing the Faith in the Indies," said Las Casas in the 22d Proposition, "should be the same as those by which Christ introduced his religion into the world, mild, peaceable and charitable," and he held that if the kings of Spain did not use the authority thus received from the Pope over the Indies for the purpose and in the manner which he stated, then they had no right to exercise such authority. In the 28th

Proposition he said that "The Devil could not have done more mischief than the Spaniards have done in spoiling the countries with their rapacity and tyranny; subjecting the natives to cruel tasks, treating them like beasts, and persecuting those especially who apply to the monks for instructions."

Las Casas described the Indians of Cuba as lambs who had encountered tigers, wolves and lions. Occasionally, he tells us, a maddened Indian would kill a Spaniard, and then his death would be followed by the massacre of a score or a hundred natives. The more generous the presents in treasures which were made by some timid Cacique to his despoilers, the more brutally was he dealt with in hope of extorting what he was suspected of having concealed. Las Casas stakes his veracity on this assertion: "I saw with my own eyes above six thousand children die in three or four months."

He had, of course, a large number of enemies, who were interested in preventing any interference in the conduct of affairs in the new world, and one of their principal arguments was that his statements were greatly exaggerated; but it is well established that although Las Casas may possibly have exaggerated somewhat the number of the victims, for he made it amount in some of his writings to even fifty millions, his tale was nevertheless entirely correct as to the cruelty of the conquerors. In one of his works he quoted a protest from the Bishop of Santa Martha, written in 1541, to the King of Spain, in which the Bishop said: "The Spaniards live there like devils, rather than Christians, violating all the laws of God and man." Herrera, who in his Historia General, published in Madrid in 1601, was the first of the historians of the new world to use documentary proofs to any extent, says that Las Casas was worthy of all confidence and in no particulars has failed to tell the truth. Even Torquemada, of infamous inquisitorial name, sustained the truth of his assertions.

His principal enemies were Oviedo, who had held high offices in the new world, and Juan Ginez de Sepulveda, a theologian and historian. The latter made two points or "Conclusions" against the "Clerigo," first, that the Spaniards had a right to subjugate and require the submission of the Indians because of their own superior wisdom and prudence, and second, that if the Indians should refuse to submit they might justly be constrained by force of arms.

Las Casas wrote a large number of memorials or argumentative treaties in refutation of the doctrines of his opponents.

His biographer, Llorente, said that he was blameless, and that there was no stain upon his great virtues. He died in Madrid in July, 1569.

SPANISH RULE IN CUBA.

(This notice on Las Casas is condensed from the extensive account of his life and works in the 2d vol. of Justin Winsor's History of America.)

4

On the 4th of December, 1860, President Buchanan sent a message to Congress in which he said that he had arrived at the conclusion that Congress had no power to coerce into submission "a state which is attempting to withdraw, or has actually withdrawn from the Confederacy."

5

Mr. Soule in a letter from Madrid to Secretary Marcy, dated June 24, 1854, referring to the proclamation of President Pierce against the filibusters, said: "It is considered by many as a disingenuous mode of masking designs which they suppose it were a scandal to lay bare to the gaze of the world," and he called that impression "strange and discrepant."

6

"Otho (the King of Greece in 1861) was a man whom the Greek people had no further use for. He had promised Victor Emanuel to organize a National Guard in Greece and he had failed to keep his word. I showed the **King of Italy that the inevitable fall of Otho was to hap-**

pen soon. 'Yes,' he said, 'all kings who do not carry out the will of their people must fall; and that one also,' he added striking with an energetical gesture the table with his fist, 'that one also will shortly fall'

"Will a day ever come when it will be necessary to remind, I will not say Victor Emanuel, but some one of his successors, of these beautiful words?"

(Marco Antonio Canini, "Vingt ans d'Exil," Paris, 1869.)

Amadeus was a son of Victor Emanuel, and a brother of Humbert, the present King of Italy.

7

Heinrich Heine said of himself:

"I am a German poet,
Of goodly German fame;"

but he lived most of his life in France, and his fame is world-wide.

The maxim quoted here is contained in a passage of his writings which, not to speak of its grim humor, originality and the sudden and unexpected transition from a calm and pastoral style to one of intense force combine to render one of the most remarkable things ever written in any language. Here it is such as I find it translated by

Richard Burton, in the "Library of the World's Best Literature:"—

"I have the most peaceful disposition. My desires are a modest cottage with thatched roof, but a good bed, good fare, fresh milk and butter, flowers by my window, and a few pine trees before the door, and if the Lord wished to fill my cup of happiness, he would grant me the pleasure of seeing some six or seven of my enemies hanged on those trees. With a heart moved to pity, I would before their death forgive the injury they had done me during their lives. Yes, we ought to forgive our enemies—but not until they are hanged."

It has been said of Heine that "he was mortified by physical infirmity and moral disappointment into a harsh and sometimes cruel satirist."

7A

"In the midst of the overbearing lordship of Spain, which was a shame to our country, and which from the treaty of Chateau-Cambrai lasted for almost a century and a half, Venice knew how to keep herself independent. To the silly Spanish bragging the aristocracy still was finding the strength of answering with a severe pride, and from **the interdict of Paul V. to the** war for the succession of Mantua the government of Saint Mark still had the courage of showing itself, alone in Italy, constantly and openly anti-Spanish."

(Pompeo Molmenti, History of Venice in private life, page 327.)

8

Since this has been written I find in Le Figaro of April 23d an excellent article in which the writer, who signs himself simply "An American," makes an appeal for a proper understanding of the situation, and states our position with great clearness and correction. He ends by saying that what France has done for the United States at the time of the Revolution—when she generously gave her blood and her gold—is exactly what we are doing now for the Cubans. The editor prefaces the article with a statement in which he says that the writer is one of the most eminent American statesmen, but that Spain has "positive right" on her side and that the sympathies of the paper will remain for her.

The eminent American statesman will not convince the "Figaro," for the reason that "il n'y a pas de pire sourd que celui qui ne veut pas entendre" (there is no greater deafness than that of the man who does not wish to hear).

9

The title of "the butcher" was also applied fifty years ago to the Austrian Marshal, Haynau, famous for the cruelties which he committed in Hungary. During a visit which he paid in September, 1850, to the great brewery of Barclay & Perkins, in Southwark, London, he was assaulted by several hundreds of the working men in that establishment. The indignant Britons threw at him trusses of straw, grain and missiles of every kind that came to hand, shouting "Down with the Austrian butcher!"

10

Justin Winsor, in his History of America, referring to the efforts made by Las Casas in his various trips to Spain in order to secure the passage of laws favorable to the Indians, says "Perhaps the same vessel or fleet which carried him to the Islands with orders intended to advance his influence would bear fellow-passengers with documents or means to thwart all his reinforced mission."

A clearer case of duplicity was never shown.

11

Maria Cristina, Archduchess of Austria, was born on the 21st of July, 1858. She married King Alfonso XII. of Spain on the 29th of November, 1879. King Alfonso died November 25th, 1885, and six months after his death Maria Cristina gave birth to a son who was named Alfonso, Leon, Ferdinand, Maria, James, Isidor, etc. On the day of his birth the little fellow was proclaimed King under the Regency of his mother.

12

Dr. F. F. Falco arrived in New York May 22, 1898. He is on his way to Cuba as a Delegate of the "Central Italian Committee for the liberation of Cuba," and he bears to President Masso the Resolutions of the Italians who are friendly to the Cuban cause.

The Resolutions are signed by several members of the Italian Chamber of Deputies, and by other Italian notabilities, among them Mrs. Adele Albani in behalf of a committee of ladies. The text of the document is as follows:

"Whereas the Cuban Committee of Rome is convinced that the revolution of Cuba has commended itself to the civilized world by the heroism of the insurgents against the long continued cruelty of their oppressors, and

"Whereas that revolution deserves the praise and approval of Rome, expressed through a decree of the People, therefor be it

"Resolved, that Cuba after having proclaimed her independence should be allowed to determine on the political form of her new existence by a popular vote, and be it further

"Resolved, that Dr. Francesco Frederic Falco, a member of this Committee, be directed to bear to the **Cuban** government a copy of these Resolutions."

Dr. Falco is also the bearer of similar resolutions which have been adopted by political associations in every part of Italy. They express sentiments of sympathy for the Cubans and for all nations and governments which may help them, and they appeal to all men to faithfully assist those who are fighting for their liberty, and "to be on their guard against the schemes of a treasonous press, which in helping Spain at the present time is forgetful of its mission of civilization." Dr. Falco says that the young men of Italy would be glad to have an opportunity of shedding their blood for the liberation of Cuba.

When the murder of Maceo occurred, the Italian Parliament was the only one of the Parliaments of Europe in which a protest was made against it.

(From the newspaper "Il Progresso Italo-Americano," New York, May 25th, 1898.)

APPENDIX.

Latest Official Statistics of the Spanish Colonies.
(From the Statesman's Year Book for 1897.)

CUBA.

Cuba is divided into six provinces, each with a capital of the same name. The Governor-General is assisted by a Council of Administration, nominated by royal decree, and the Island is represented in the Spanish Parliament by 16 senators and 30 deputies. The pretended Autonomist system, recently introduced, modifies somewhat the constitutional intercourse between the Island and the mother-country. Ten per cent. of the area is cultivated, 7 per cent. is unreclaimed, and 4 per cent. is under forests. There are large tracts of country still unexplored. The population of the Island in 1894 was given as 1,631,696, of which 65 per cent. was white, the remainder being negro. A law passed in 1886 abolished slavery absolutely. The capital, Havana, has (December, 1887) 198,271 inhabitants, and the other most important towns are Santiago de Cuba, 71,307; Matanzas (1892), 27,000; Cienfuegos (1892), 27,430; Puerto Principe, 46,641; Holguin, 34,767; Sancti Spiritu, 32,608; Cardenas (1892) 23,-

SPANISH RULE IN CUBA. 211

680. Education was made obligatory in 1880. There are 843 public schools in the Island, and Havana has a university.

The estimated revenue for 1893-94, was 24,440,759 pesos, of which 11,375,000 was from customs; expenditure, 25,-984,239 pesos, of which 12,574,485 pesos was for the debt, 5,904,084 pesos for the Ministry of War, and 4,015,034 pesos for the Ministry of the Interior. The debt, which is rapidly increasing, is put at about 200,000,000 pesos. (The value of the gold "peso" is 93 cents American money.)

The number of landed estates on the island in 1892 was estimated at 90,960 of the value of 220,000,000 pesos, and rental of 17,000,000 pesos. The live stock consisted of 584,725 horses and mules, 2,485,766 cattle, 78,494 sheep, and 570,194 pigs. The chief produce is sugar and tobacco. The quantity of sugar produced in the year 1892-93, was 815,894 tons; in 1893-94, 1,054,214 tons; 1894-95, 1,004,264 tons. Of 832,431 tons of sugar exported in 1895, 769,962 tons went to the United States. The insurrection and incendiarism in the island ruined the prospects of sugar cultivation since 1896. The export of tobacco in 1892 was 241,291 bales; 1893, 227,865 bales. The number of Havana cigars exported in 1892 was 154,931,133; in 1893, 147,365,-000; in 1894, 134,210,000; in 1895, 156,513,000. Cigarettes exported in 1895, 48,163,846 packets. Nearly all the tobacco and nearly half of the cigars go to the United States. Mahogany and other timbers are exported, as are also honey, wax, and fruits. The total exports from Cuba in 1892 amounted to 89,652,514 pesos, of which 84,964,685 pesos was for vegetable, 871,625 pesos for animal, and 3,485,924 pesos for mineral produce. The import value was put at 56,265,315 pesos, of which 18,553,307 pesos was from Spain, 16,245, 880 pesos from the United States, and 13,051,384 from Great Britain. The chief imports are rice, jerked beef, and flour. The Spanish official returns state the value of the imports from Cuba into Spain for 1894 to be 37,643,110 Spanish pesetas, and the exports from Spain to Cuba 117,061,881 pesetas.

In the district of Santiago de Cuba, at the end of 1891, the total number of mining titles issued was 296, with an extent of 13,727 hectares. Of the mines reported and claimed, 138 were iron, 88 manganese, and 53 copper. In 1895 the port of Havana was visited by 1,179 vessels of 1,691,325 tons; Cienfuegos and Cardenas by 490 of 645,184 tons, and Santiago de Cuba by 338 of 462,888 tons. In Cuba there are about 1,000 miles of railway belonging to companies, and the larger sugar estates have private lines connecting them with the main lines. There are 2,300 miles of telegraph line with 153 offices. Messages in 1893, 342,331.

PORTO RICO.

Porto Rico is described as "the healthiest of all the Antilles." The population, December 31, 1887, was 813,937. The negro population is estimated at over 300,000. Slavery was abolished in 1873. Chief town, San Juan, 23,414 inhabitants; Ponce 37,545; San German, 30,146. The Porto Rico budget for 1893-94 gave an estimated expenditure of 3,879,813 pesos, of which the Ministry of Finance absorbed 250,045 pesos, and the Ministry of War 1,050,000 pesos, and an estimated income of 3,903,655 pesos, of which the customs were estimated to produce 2,300,000 pesos, and direct and indirect taxes 1,358,800 pesos. The principal articles of exports in 1895 were coffee, 16,884 tons (value $8,779,655); sugar, 54,861 tons ($3,560,655); tobacco, 1,807 tons ($763,610). The total exports in 1893 amounted to $16,745,390, and imports to $17,320,450. The value of the imports from Porto Rico into Spain in 1894 was 21,580,125 Spanish pesetas (a peseta equals 19 cents American money), and the exports from Spain to Porto Rico 28,678,899 pesetas. In 1893, 1,034 vessels of 1,008,581 tons entered, and 999 vessels of 902,095 tons, cleared Porto Rico.

In Porto Rico there are 470 miles of telegraph and 137 miles of railway, besides over 170 miles under construction.

In Porto Rico, the coin in use is the 5-pesetas piece.

The coinage of Spanish dollars of similar value, to take their place, has been decreed.

PHILIPPINE ISLANDS.

These islands extend almost due north and south from Formosa to Borneo and the Moluccas, embracing an extent of 16 degrees of latitude and 9 degrees of longitude. They are over 400 in number; the two largest are Luzon (area 40,024 square miles) and Mindanao. The capital of the Philippines, Manila, has 154,062 inhabitants (1887); other towns are Laog, 30,642; Lipa, 43,408; Banang, 35,598; Batangas, 35,587. There is a small resident Spanish population, but a large number of Chinese. The native inhabitants are mostly of the Malayan race, but there are some tribes of Negritos. The Government is administered by a governor-general and a captain-general, and the 43 provinces are ruled by governors, alcaldes, or commandants, according to their importance and position.

The estimated revenue of the Philippine Islands in 1894-95 was $13,600,000 and expenditure $13,200,000. There is an export duty on tobacco, and almost every article of foreign production is heavily taxed on being imported. On muslins and petroleum the duty is about 100 per cent. of the cost.

The chief products are hemp, sugar, coffee, copra, tobacco-leaf, cigars, indigo. Gold mining is being carried on in Luzon with favorable prospects, and coal mining in

SPANISH RULE IN CUBA.

Cebu, where, when arrangements for carriage are completed, the output is expected to be about 5,000 tons per month.

In 1894, the total imports were valued at 28,530,000 dollars; and exports at 33,250,000 dollars. In 1895, the chief exports were: hemp, 832,322 bales (1 bale equals about 2½ cwt), valued at $8,325,000; sugar, 230,083 tons, valued at $6,025,000; copra, 61,438 piculs, valued at $1,405,000; tobacco-leaf, 207,371 quintals; cigars, 164,430,000; coffee, 194 tons. Owing to disease the production of coffee is falling off. The chief imports are rice, flour, wines, dress, petroleum, coal. In 1895, 177,620 piculs of rice were imported from Hong Kong, Saigon, and Singapore; 61,391 tons of coal from Australia and Japan; 357,538 cases of petroleum. On an average about 34 per cent. of the import value is from the United Kingdom, 21 per cent. from Hong Kong and Amoy, 13 per cent. from Spain, and 10 per cent. from Singapore and British India. Imports into Spain from the Philippine Islands in 1894, 17,994,838 pesetas; exports to Philippine Islands, 28,584,122 pesetas. In 1895 304 vessels of 425,025 tons cleared the ports of Manila, Iloilo, and Cebu. There are 720 miles of telegraph in the islands, and 70 miles of railway.

The coin in use is the Mexican dollar with locally coined fractional money. The import of foreign money is illegal, but that of Mexican dollars is permitted.

WEATHER OF CUBA.

Temperature.—The average annual temperature of Havana, as determined from the observations at Belen College, Havana, made during the decennium 1888-1897, may be stated in round numbers as 77° F. In this decennium the highest annual temperature was 77.2°, and this occurred upon three occasions; and the lowest annual temperature was 76.1°, and happened upon only one occasion, showing in the ten years an extreme range in annual averages of but 1.1° F. It would therefore, seem probable that the mean temperature for the decennial period 1888-1897 is about a true average for Havana for any long period. The warmest month at Havana is July, with an average temperature of 82.4° F. The warmest July in this decennium had an average temperature of 83.5° F., and the coolest July a temperature of 81.7° F. The warmest single month in the decennial period was August, 1888, when the average temperature was 84.2° F. The coldest month is January, with an average temperature of 70.3° F., and the warmest and coldest Januaries in this decennium were, respectively, 73.4° F. and 67.5° F. The highest temperature recorded was 100.6° F. in July, 1891, and the lowest, 49.6° F. in February, 1896.

For Matanzas, on the coast about 50 miles east of Havana, there is a record for two years, beginning in August, 1832, and ending in July, 1833, and again beginning in January, 1835, and ending with December of the same year. From this record the mean annual temperature at Matanzas appears to be about 78°. The highest temperature is recorded as 93°, and the lowest as 51°.

At Santiago, on the extreme southeast coast, the temperature is apparently higher than on the northern and western coasts, and from the meager data available appears to be about 80°, with an average difference between the warmest and coldest months of about 6° F.

ATMOSPHERIC MOISTURE.

Relative Humidity.—The relative humidity of the atmosphere appears to be fairly constant, as far as can be determined from the observations available. It averages about 75 per cent. of saturation. The mean relative humidity of the different months differs hardly enough to characterize one month as being drier or damper than another.

From observations made at Havana at different hours of the day, it appears that the diurnal range of the relative humidity is considerable, varying from a maximum of about 88 per cent. in the morning to a minimum of about 64 per cent. at noon.

Absolute Humidity.—The absolute humidity is very great. At Havana the average is about 7.5 grains of vapor to the cubic foot of air. The absolute humidity varies from 6.2 grains per cubic foot in January to 8.9 grains in September.

RAINFALL.

The rainfall shows to a greater degree than the temperature the influence of locality and season of the year. The average rainfall for Havana is about 52 inches for the year.

Observations have probably been taken continuously at Belen College Observatory since 1859, but the records on file in the Library of the Weather Bureau show a hiatus from 1876 to 1884, inclusive. In the combined periods, 1859–75 and 1885–97, the greatest annual rainfall was 71.40 inches in 1867, and the smallest fall was 40.59 inches in 1861. The average rainfall for the thirty years was 51.73 inches.

The rainy season at Havana begins in the latter part of May and the first of June and ends with October. Relatively the greater bulk of the rain falls during the months from June to October. The average rainfall for this period is 32.37 inches, or 63 per cent. of the annual fall.

STORMS.

Thunderstorms, with much electrical display, are of frequent or almost daily occurrence, but little damage results from them. The West Indies are more or less subject during each summer to one or more severe tropical storms or hurricanes. These storms are more likely to occur in the months of August, September and October.

WEATHER OF MANILA.

Manila, the capital and chief port of the Philippine Islands, is situated in latitude 14° 35′ north, and in longitude 121° east of Greenwich.

Meteorological observations have been made for many years at the Observatorio Meteorologico de Manila. Observations of rainfall for thirty-two consecutive years, and of other meteorological elements for seventeen consecutive years, have been published by the Observatory.

Temperature. — The average temperature of the year is 80° F. The months of April, May, and June are the hottest part of the year. May, with an average temperature of 84° F., is the hottest of the three. December and January are the coolest months, each with an average temperature of 77° F. The highest thermometer reading recorded is 100° F; this was observed in May. The lowest reading recorded is 74°, and was observed in January.

Humidity.—The average relative humidity is 78 per cent. That of the most humid month, which is September, is 85 per cent., and that of the least humid month, which is April, is 70 per cent. The average absolute humidity is 8.75 grains in a cubic foot. It is greatest in August and least in February.

Rainfall.— The average annual rainfall is 75.43 inches, of which 43.69 inches, more than 57 per cent., fall during the months of July, August and September, and 50.74 inches, more than 80 per cent., fall from June to October, inclusive. September has the largest average fall, 15.01 inches, and February the smallest average fall, 0.47 inches. The heaviest rainfall in any one month was 61.43 inches in September, and sometimes no rain at all has fallen in February, March, April and May.

Departures from the average rainfall are in some instances remarkable. For example, as much as 120.98 inches have fallen in one year, and as little as 35.65 inches in another. Still more remarkable was the fall of 61.43 inches in one September, and that of only 2.00 inches in another September.

www.ingramcontent.com/pod-product-compliance
Lightning Source LLC
Chambersburg PA
CBHW031813230426
43669CB00009B/1122